# THOMAS HARDY

## THE FORMS OF TRAGEDY

# Thomas Hardy

# The Forms of Tragedy

by DALE KRAMER

UNIVERSITY OF ILLINOIS

WAYNE STATE UNIVERSITY PRESS, DETROIT, 1975

*Second printing, August 1976.*

*Kramer, Dale, 1936-*
    *Thomas Hardy: the forms of tragedy.*

    *Includes bibliographical references.*
    *1. Hardy, Thomas, 1840-1928 — Criticism and inter-*
*pretation.   2. Tragedy.   I. Title.*
*PR4754.K7        823'.8        74-17084*
*ISBN 0-8143-1530-5*

*Publication of this book was assisted by*
*the American Council of Learned*
*Societies under a grant from the*
*Andrew W. Mellon Foundation.*

*For*

*Frances*

*Cheris*

*Brinlee*                    *Jana*

# CONTENTS

# ACKNOWLEDGMENTS

To my colleagues Donald Smalley and Jack Stillinger, both of whom read the manuscript in its early stages and gave encouragement and useful criticism, I wish to express my thanks. Cheris Kramer helped to correct the manuscript in the early drafts, and my students at Ohio University and the University of Illinois have contributed ideas and have assisted me in arriving at my interpretations and in correcting some errors of emphasis. Funds to cover some of the expenses in preparing the manuscript were provided by the Graduate College Research Board at the University of Illinois.

Permission to publish material from the Hardy novels that are still in copyright has been granted by the Trustees of the Hardy Estate, The Macmillan Company of Canada Limited, and Macmillan of London and Basingstoke. Part of the first chapter was published in *The Dalhousie Review* (1971), vol. 51, and is reprinted here with the permission of the Dalhousie University Press Limited. Approximately half of the chapter on *The Mayor of Casterbridge* appeared in *Tennessee Studies in Literature,* ed. Richard Beale Davis and Kenneth L. Knickerbocker (1971), vol. 16 (Copyright, © 1971 by the University of Tennessee Press), and is reprinted here with the permission of the University of Tennessee Press.

*Textual Note*

Quotations from Hardy's novels are from the Wessex edition (London: Macmillan, 1912), or from reissues of this edition termed the Library edition and the Greenwood edition. Page references to these editions which are identical are given in the text. I have altered the punctuation of dialogue to conform with customary American usage so that the punctuation of long passages is consistent with that of brief quotations within my own sentences. References to Hardy's memoirs, or autobiography, are also within the text: *The Early Life of Thomas Hardy, 1840-1891* (London: Macmillan, 1928) is cited as *Early Life;* *The Later Years of Thomas Hardy, 1892-1928* (London: Macmillan, 1930) is cited as *Later Years.* The memoirs were written by Hardy in the third person and published after his death under the name of his second wife. For an account of the autobiography, see Richard Little Purdy, *Thomas Hardy: A Bibliographical Study* (1954; reprint ed., Oxford: Clarendon Press; New York: Oxford University Press, 1968), pp. 265-67, 272-73.

# 1

# INTRODUCTION

The crucial role that form or structure plays in the novelist's presentation of life was obvious to Thomas Hardy. His novels are carefully constructed; and the once fashionable observation that his architectural training as a youth was the reason he built neat, geometric plots does not account for the range of experimentation and inventiveness in the forms of his novels. Hardy's continuing popularity has to do with a combination of seriousness, tenderness, and tolerance that enables him to make significant interpretations of experience. The structural features of his novels are not usually noticed either by general readers or by critics, even though structure is a dominant factor in creating the tragic qualities of the individual novels. My interest is to suggest some of the ways the forms Hardy employed in his great novels contribute to his achievement of tragedy.

The rarity of studies of the structure of Hardy's work is surprising,[1] but not difficult to explain. Both critics and their readers soon became wearied by demonstrations that Hardy's mechanical plots were masterpieces of organization. Rigid character alignments like those in *Far from the Madding Crowd* have lost their appeal, and few readers have attempted to see more subtle manifestations of structural technique in Hardy. Albert Guerard, a well-known modern critic of Hardy, reverts to old standards long enough to admire the structure of *The Mayor of Casterbridge* and *Under the Greenwood Tree*, but otherwise condemns Hardy's novels as "radically imperfect in structure."[2] The disinclination to apply rigorous analysis to Hardy's novels is the natural result of a strong prejudice still lingering that Hardy was a simple man and that his books are straightforward and often awkward, and therefore must be as structurally innovative as children's tales (which of course are often more innovative than careless opinion allows).

Still, this lacuna in Hardy studies is ironic. Hardy could reasonably have expected his employment of form to be examined as exhaustively as any other aspect of his work. Certainly, he was more conscious of the qualities of the forms of his works than he was of their "philosophy." He always insisted that he was a philosophical impressionist, eschewing responsibility as a thinker. But he took the shape of his books seriously. His primary criterion for judging a fellow novelist is form. He praises Anatole France as one "who never forgets the value of organic form and symmetry" (*Later Years,* p. 159), and admires the "construction" of Trollope's *Eustace Diamonds.*[3] He extolls the first thirty chapters of *Vanity Fair* as "well-nigh complete in artistic presentation," and *The Bride of Lammermoor* as "an almost perfect specimen of form," superior to the lauded *Tom Jones.*[4] He holds his age in scorn because it is not interested in form: in the same passage in *Later Years* in which he praises Anatole France, he describes the times (1913) as "these days when the literature of narrative and verse seems to be losing its qualities as an art, and to be assuming a structureless and conglomerate character." About 1920, he wryly notes that the *Saturday Review* called *A Pair of Blue Eyes* "the most artistically constructed of the novels of its time [1873] — a quality which, by the bye, would carry little recommendation in these days of loose construction and indifference to organic homogeneity" (*Early Life,* p. 126). He remarks upon the "simplicity" of Bible narrative as "the simplicity of the highest cunning" and adds, "One is led to inquire, when even in these latter days artistic development and arrangement are the qualities least appreciated by readers, who was there likely to appreciate the art in these chronicles at that day?" (*Early Life,* pp. 222-23). Hardy's objection to the tastes of his age is grounded in an abhorrence of the results of literary realism.[5] In 1891 he criticizes William Dean Howells "and those of his school" for forgetting that a story must be striking (*Early Life,* p. 314); and he says in 1897 that he stopped writing serials "with all the less reluctance in that the novel was, in [Hardy's] own words, 'gradually losing artistic form, with a beginning, middle, and end, and becoming a spasmodic inventory of items, which has nothing to do with art'" (*Later Years,* p. 65).

The key word in Hardy's comments on form in fiction would seem to be *organic.* Everything affecting the plot and characters must be natural to the conditions in the novel and must grow out of those conditions. Hardy's admission that he made no effort in *The Dynasts* to be organic indicates something of his idea of the concept:

> No attempt has been made to create that completely organic structure of action, and closely-webbed development of character and motive, which are demanded in a drama strictly self-contained. A panoramic show like the present is a series of historical "ordinates" (to use a term in geometry): the subject is familiar to all; and foreknowledge is assumed to fill in the junctions required to combine the scenes into an artistic unity.[6]

Although he criticizes himself for damaging *The Mayor of Casterbridge* "as an artistic whole" by including an incident in each week's serial plot, he adds that the plot "was quite coherent and organic, in spite of its complication." One look at this entire passage shows how contorted Hardy's syntax becomes when he refers to his indifference to fiction, as if he were torn by equally strong urges to affirm and to deny the dedication he had given to his writing decades before he came to write his autobiography:

> *The Mayor of Casterbridge*...was a story which Hardy fancied he had damaged more recklessly as an artistic whole, in the interest of the newspaper in which it appeared serially, than perhaps any other of his novels, his aiming to get an incident into almost every week's part causing him in his own judgment to add events to the narrative somewhat too freely. However, as at this time he called his novel-writing "mere journeywork" he cared little about it as art, though it must be said in favour of the plot, as he admitted later, that it was quite coherent and organic, in spite of its complication. [*Early Life,* p. 235]

In "The Profitable Reading of Fiction," his longest statement of his idea of form in fiction, Hardy argues that there is a "beauty of shape" in fiction that gives a pleasure equal to that gained from pleasing shapes in pictures or sculpture:

> Briefly, a story should be an organism. To use the words applied to the epic by Addison, whose artistic feeling in this kind was of the subtlest, "nothing should go before it, be intermixed with it, or follow after it, that is not related to it." [7]

Hardy's frame of reference in these remarks is obviously Aristotle's dictum that the art work should contain a beginning, a middle, and an end; but it includes more than the bare features of neat relevance. It includes, as does Aristotle's outline of dramatic principles, the necessity that all narrative devices be appropriate to the plot, atmosphere, and final significance.

Hardy's interest in the naturalness, or organic nature, of the form of fiction is reflected in his remarks on style. The simplicity of his prose is a deliberate quality which he sought to achieve following a study of both punctilious and casual stylists — Addison, Macaulay, Newman, Sterne, Defoe, Lamb, Gibbon, and Burke. From these writers Hardy learned that "the whole secret of a living style and the difference between it and a dead style, lies in not having too much style — being — in fact, a little careless, or rather seeming to be, here and there"(*Early Life,* p. 138). Early in his career he imitates "the affected simplicity of Defoe's" in its "naive realism in circumstantial details" and in its "affected simplicity of the narrative" (*Early Life,* pp. 81, 82). We have already noted that Hardy's admiration of the so-called simplicity of the Bible narratives recognizes that it is, ironically, "the simplicity of the highest cunning." A skeptical reader may feel that Hardy in his creative writing did not maintain consistently a successful balance between "carelessness" and deliberateness. But more importantly, his autobiography reveals that at every period in his career, although he seldom theorized at length about style, he was conscious of theoretical aesthetics. "The Profitable Reading of Fiction" presents a view of style more modern than conservative, certainly not that of the traditional ballad-maker (whom Hardy is often thought to resemble), who finds little room for self-expression because of the restrictions of the form itself:

The indefinite word style may be made to express almost any characteristic of story-telling other than subject and plot, and it is too commonly
viewed as being some independent, extraneous virtue or varnish with
which the substance of a narrative is artificially overlaid. Style, as far
as the word is meant to express something more than literary finish, can
only be treatment, and treatment depends upon the mental attitude of
the novelist; thus entering into the very substance of a narrative, as into
that of any other kind of literature. A writer who is not a mere imitator
looks upon the world with his personal eyes, and in his peculiar moods;
thence grows up his style, in the full sense of the term.

> Cui lecta potenter erit res,
> Nec facundia deseret hunc, nec lucidus ordo.[8]

Those who would profit from the study of style should formulate
an opinion of what it consists in by the aid of their own educated understanding, their perception of natural fitness, true and high feeling, sin-
cerity, unhampered by considerations of nice collocation and balance
of sentences, still less by conventionally accepted examples.[9]

Hardy seems not to have viewed himself as a throwback to an
earlier age of storytelling, as many of his readers have. At least, he
explicitly admonishes that art must progress. "What has been written
cannot be blotted. Each new style of novel must be the old with added
ideas, not an ignoring and avoidance of the old" (*Early Life,* p. 285).
Nor would Hardy settle for attempts to repeat previous methods; he
remarks in 1906 that he especially admires the successful artist who
is "not contented with the grounds of his success" and goes on to attempt more difficult tasks (*Later Years,* p. 117); and he points out that
easy success is less meaningful than an arduous risk that fails. "Critics can never be made to understand that the failure may be greater
than the success. It is their particular duty to point this out; but the
public points it out to them. To have strength to roll a stone weighing
a hundredweight to the top of the mount is a success, and to have the
strength to roll a stone of ten hundredweight only half-way up that
mount is a failure. But the latter is two or three times as strong a
deed" (*Later Years,* p. 123). These brief quotations attest that critics
who are disposed to quote Hardy's diffident remarks sloughing off his
fiction are only noting part of Hardy's attitude. It is true that he observed coolly in 1887 that finishing *The Woodlanders* that year "en-
abled me to hold my own in fiction, whatever that may be worth"

(*Early Life,* p. 267); but his best-known demurral of lofty ambition, his remarks in 1874 to his editor Leslie Stephen that he wished "merely to be considered a good hand at a serial," is usually quoted incompletely. The full sentence in Hardy's letter reads, "Perhaps I may have higher aims some day, and be a great stickler for the proper artistic balance of the completed work, but *for the present* circumstances lead me to wish merely to be considered a good hand at a serial" (*Early Life,* p. 131; my italics). The circumstances included his desire to have a secure enough income to enable him to marry Emma Lavinia Gifford, an income which was ensured by the success of the serial he was working on at the time he made the remark, *Far from the Madding Crowd.* (A comment following the above quotation refers obliquely but unmistakably to the coming marriage.)

The indebtedness to Aristotle in Hardy's preference for a plot with a beginning, a middle, and an end calls to mind the tragic connotations that his art evokes. But though *The Mayor of Casterbridge* is modeled to a large degree on Aristotle and though Hardy attempted to employ the unities of time and place in *The Return of the Native,* he does not adhere consistently to Aristotle's ideas on tragedy or to those of any clearly defined school. Indeed, the terms under which Hardy can be considered a tragedian have always been rather problematic.

The kinds of argument used to evaluate Hardy's tragic art have overlapped chronologically, but there have also been identifiable trends. A sketch of the most distinctive of these trends will take us a good distance into the permanent strengths of Hardy as commentator on life and experience, and allow us to see how pertinent his works are to modern efforts to define the tragic vision.

Hardy throughout his lifetime and for sometime thereafter was called tragic by critics who were concentrating upon the grandeur of his conceptions, the lowering gloom of his characteristic atmospheres, and the courage of his characters who are unable to avoid being destroyed by Fate or Chance.[10] In the twenties and thirties an interest in the spirit of science brought approval to Hardy by critics who saw his plots "in terms suggestive of physics and dynamics"; the dominant position of A.C. Bradley in Shakespearean criticism and a simplistic Aristotelianism encouraged readers of Hardy to consider the first five books of *The Return of the Native* like "the five acts of a classic play."[11] With the rise of rhetorical criticism and the demand for formal unity—two results of the rigorous scanning performed on individual works by the New Critics—Hardy's star as tragic writer declined precipitously because his techniques that previously had drawn praise were scorned for their ineptness. Bareness of motivation, rough-hewn and mechanical plots that lumber to what seem to be predetermined conclusions, commitment to a certain philosophy—these accusations have debased his currency.[12]

But the same New Criticism which contributed to Hardy's decline is also responsible for a rejuvenation of interest in the *tragic* as a quality in literature apart from the manner in which certain pieces of writing employ methods that are present in classical masterpieces. Critics who have applied New Criticism standards to generic investigation have located the "vision" or "spirit" of tragedy not in classical or Elizabethan forms alone but in recurrent concerns that the *substance* of the work possesses. Ironically, this sort of analytical criticism is far kinder to Hardy than the sort that demands total linguistic cohesion, which the school of New Criticism, from which these tragic theorists spring, had demanded before awarding its gold stars.

Joseph Wood Krutch's regretful but unceremonious attempt in 1929 to bury tragedy as an active genre in the modern world is probably responsible for the formulation of many of the recent theories defending the existence of tragedy. Krutch does not refer to Hardy in his essay, "The Tragic Fallacy";[13] but ironically Hardy comes close to supplying an example of the potentiality of tragedy in modern times. To use Krutch's terms, Hardy believes in man even if he cannot believe in God. Although Krutch considers modern tragedy debilitated because man can no longer look upon himself as the center of a universe governed by meaningful laws, Jude, Tess, Eustacia, and Henchard each experiences in his or her death "one of those splendid calamities which in Shakespeare seem to reverberate through the universe." Although Hardy's universe is a calamitous place in which to exist, his protagonists are equal to the demands. Tess shows an ability to suffer "more than [she] can bear," Eustacia commits suicide rather than give in to the pressures of the universe to become less than a "splendid woman," and Jude kills himself in defiance of a life made

empty by Sue's apostasy. Hardy considers the existence of his characters to have importance; they may be desolate but they are never, to
use Krutch's term, mean.

And in an oddly paradoxical way, the protagonist of a novel by
Hardy does live — as Krutch insists a tragic hero should — in a "world
which he may not dominate but which is always aware of him," though
it is a truism that Hardy's universal forces are unconscious and thus
think no more of man than of plants. Despite its ostensible uncon-
sciousness, Hardy's universe operates in such a way that man does become its center, its measuring device. Hardy remarks in *The Mayor of
Casterbridge* that man is always superior to his environment, and thus
no man receives less than he deserves. And as Roy Morrell has dem-
onstrated in *Thomas Hardy: The Will and the Way*,[14] Hardy's characteristic protagonist follows a course that shows his life "not to be
merely an accusation against . . . [but] a justification of, the world in
which it occurs."[15]   Foolishness and failure to act cause tragedy in
*Tess of the d'Urbervilles* and *Jude the Obscure,* a refusal to look at
the truth causes disaster in *The Return of the Native,* choices made in
*The Woodlanders* tangle its lives and actions, and *The Mayor of Casterbridge* traces the career of a man impelled by his very character to
take actions the least advantageous to himself. Thus Hardy's protagonists merit their fates and justify to man the ways of the universe. His
novels satisfy "the universally human desire to find in the world some
justice, some meaning, or, at the very least, some recognizable order,"
though that order and justice may be uncongenial and harsh, assessing
cruel punishment for a minor misstep; with the possible exception of
*Jude the Obscure,* each Hardy novel, like every "real tragedy, however tremendous it may be, is an affirmation of faith in life, a declaration that even if God is not in his Heaven, then at least Man is in his
world."[16]   The death of Tess especially affirms this: Tess accepts her
fate as just, and so does Angel; yet Angel goes on with 'Liza-Lu to
find a life for themselves, perhaps together.

If we are to apply definitions of tragedy in a hard-and-fast manner, however, Hardy might be excluded from Krutch's definition because of his view that the higher mental life, the Immanent Will, is
unconscious (although the operation of the Will is not greatly different from that of Fate or of the gods in *King Lear*). William Van
O'Connor, another theorist skeptical like Krutch about the possibil-

ities of tragedy in the modern age, combines historical and substantive arguments. "If a glance at individualism in Greece and Elizabethan England indicates serious defects in our [modern, non-tragical] society one at least is this: individualism has been either unrestricted or all but totally repressed. There has been no sustained effort to cultivate restricted individualism that in its flowering rises above mind to spirit. Dramatic tragedy has not flourished in any other soil." [17] But Hardy fares rather well under O'Connor's jurisdiction, just as he does with Krutch. Certainly Hardy tills the "ideal" soil for tragedy: restricted individualism. His characters have "freedom," but a freedom modified by external circumstances, such as the moral codes of the society, the necessity to submit to natural powers to gain a measure of happiness and repose, and the restrictions imposed on action by the similarly free but "restricted" choices of other characters.[18] It is less clear whether Hardy deals with the flowering of restricted individualism that O'Connor looks to; Hardy's genius lies as much with the concrete, even though symbolic and expansive, as with the subtly intellectual or the "spirit." Still, the central expression of *Tess of the d'Urbervilles* is the sanctity of spirit; and *The Mayor of Casterbridge* and perhaps *Jude the Obscure* and *The Return of the Native* as well produce the sense of incommunicable depths of personality.

Among recent theories about tragedy, the most stimulating and in some ways the most challenging in its application to Hardy is that of Richard B. Sewall. Sewall's central criterion for tragedy is that the universals in conflict in the work of art must remain in perpetual and ambiguous tension — not in a state of balance, as Meyers has argued,[19] and certainly not in a resolvable form. What the tragic writer imparts is his sense of ineluctable bafflement at the true conditions of life even while he is most aware of them: to make judgments is to simplify, and thus to falsify.[20]

This paraphrase of Sewall's idea would appear on the face of it to exclude Hardy from any possible Sewall canon of tragic writers. For if a century of journalistic and academic writing about Hardy has given us nothing else, it has given us the assumption that he is a writer of "ideas," who wants to persuade readers of the adequacy or even superiority of his versions of social law and "divine" justice. But in the principal novels, Hardy manages his art so that the ideas themselves are constantly under fire. They are presented with irony, modified and even shown false by the contexts in which they occur, or contradicted by the outcome of the novels. Hardy is indeed a writer of doctrines, but he is not a simple writer of simple doctrines. Rather, his skepticism extends to himself as much as to others. It is commonly forgotten that Hardy is primarily an artist, not a propagandist. It is because Hardy was aware of the difference that he became furious and discouraged when people insisted on tagging him with a pseudo-philosophical label, such as pessimist or fatalist. He frankly and repeatedly denied claims to intellectual consistency, declaring in the prefaces to *Late Lyrics and Earlier, Tess of the d'Urbervilles*, and *Jude the Obscure* that he wrote not "convictions" but "a series of seemings, or personal impressions," which he "never tried to co-ordinate." Thus, Hardy's reliance upon impressions allows him to produce the "tensions of tragedy," which are difficult to sustain,[21] simply by following his natural inclinations.[22] His nature tends toward universal skepticism — skepticism about the meaning of *bad* as well of *good*, and the tension remains irresolvable. Even in *Jude the Obscure*, when Jude's despair about his personal life prevails over his intelligence, the tension is maintained because the personal despair is not borne out by his glimpse fifty years into the future. On the other hand, the optimism implicit in this prognosis is severely qualified by the immediate evidence that a person as worthy as Jude has made very little progress toward the presumably attainable better life.

Sewall like Krutch emphasizes the affirmation that arises through tragedy and — though conceding that Hardy's work offers "genuine tragic values" because it does not fall into "dispiriting cynicism" — believes that Hardy's "view of man's fate fell too far short of the full tragic affirmation to warrant calling [his] novels tragedies."[23] He quotes Hardy's "error and chance rule the world, not justice" to support his argument that Hardy saw little value in suffering. But this is a typically denigrative, narrow prose summary by Hardy of his own richly quizzical creative insight. Characteristically, he modifies this formula elsewhere (*Later Years*, p. 128: "neither Chance nor Purpose governs the universe, but Necessity"). And Hardy's protagonists *are* made aware by their experiences of the great questions of existence that all tragedians pose,[24] which, along with the demonstration of suffering — giving point to them — are as germane a component of tragedy as are the positive implications of the writer's total world view.[25]

Most modern theories of tragedy assume, implicitly or explicitly, that intensity is a crucial quality in the tragic personae. Unless the protagonist can feel deeply, and unless the author is able to make us realize that the protagonist is feeling deeply and suffering keenly, we are unlikely to become involved enough to catch a glimpse of the nature of existence that propels the protagonist. There is no limit to the methods by which the author can create this intensity, and so the stress placed on this point does not constitute advocacy of one facet of tragedy over another: tragedy of character over tragedy of plot or tragedy of circumstance. In Hardy the intensity of a character's perception of his situation is the principal bolstering factor in his expression of an element of tragic existence. Indeed, without this factor we could not begin to take Eustacia seriously as a challenger of nature's enigma, much less as a character intended to create empathy; it is almost solely the intensity of Tess's consciousness that makes her more than a Chance-blasted milkmaid.

The novels by Hardy taken as a whole are distinguished by their display of learning and their simple directness of narration, a combination responsible for the aura of sophisticated folklore that Hardy often achieves. They also suggest an environment compatible with the momentousness of tragedy. These conditions differ sharply from those of Conrad and Faulkner, two modern novelists who have attempted, and in varying degrees succeeded in composing, tragic fictions. Their subtleties of style and presentation of philosophies evoke more complex reactions than Hardy's qualities, although it has been argued that subtleties such as theirs diffuse rather than encourage reader involvement and that their characters and situations are too individualized to achieve the kind of reader abandonment of self that is needed for the profound empathy of tragedy.[26]

The provocativeness of Hardy's attempt to write tragedies is suggested by the perennially enlarged body of literature on "the tragic novelist Thomas Hardy." Although studies of Hardy's ideas about and use of form and structure are few, the same cannot be said about studies on the quality of tragedy in his work. From the first book on Hardy, by Lionel Johnson, nearly every book-length examination of his work has commented on tragedy, as have numerous contemporary reviews and subsequent articles. Certainly not lacking are general theories to explain what evokes the tragic atmosphere characteristic of Hardy. To the most able of these — parts of Beach's book, John Paterson's *"The Mayor of Casterbridge* as Tragedy," and Harvey Curtis Webster's rebuttal to Paterson[27] —future critics will be greatly indebted, for they provide important clarifications of Hardy's achievements.

But even with the numerous studies on Hardy's tragedy, and the efforts to relate Hardy to traditional views of tragedy — classical, Elizabethan, biblical, naturalistic — much has been left unsaid. Alterations in mood or in handling of subject; the idea of a sequential development in tragic characters, situations, and settings, from the first to the last tragic novel; experimentation in technique; explanations for the tragedies manqués — all these matters remain unresolved, and some of them unexplored or even unnoticed in readers' and critics' fascination with more exotic matters. The *form* of Hardy's tragic novels has largely gone unexplored; their classification by Beach as "chronicle," "cinematic," and "dramatic" is enlightening and stimulating but of only partial help in understanding them. Fascinated by Hardy's early training and career as an architect, Lionel Johnson and Lascelles Abercrombie praise Hardy's novels for "the form given to the material." But Johnson makes only general comments about "unity of effect" and "unity of design"; and Abercrombie deals, intelligently but abstractly, with the metaphysical relation between reality and imagination, and with "shapeliness" and "symmetry."[28] Broad classifications indicate general qualities but overlook the finer features of form that ultimately determine reader reaction and the unique effects of the individual novels.

I shall attempt to examine in this study the effects of Hardy's management of form upon his tragedies. Hardy was an experimenter in fiction as much as in poetry. And while he is not a "fine" or precise writer in the manner of James or Proust, his effects are — taken altogether — intentional. His sober presentation of human plight is not the inchoate outburst of a rustic genius but the ingrained reactions to the world of an artist who recognized his alienating vision, whose insight into individuals' situations carries his readers beyond the seemingly limited horizons of the stark prose, and whose skill at structuring his works enhances the insights and the rugged honesty of his projection of the world. Hardy wrote one successful "classical" tragedy, *The Mayor of Casterbridge;* and the authority of tone and variety of subject of his other novels suggest both conscious experimentation with and exploitation of technique and form, and an inherent vision and quality of mind communicable through different forms. The choosing of particular forms inescapably leads to certain effects not entirely desirable in the individual novels — for example, the low tension in *The Woodlanders,* the sense of disorientation in *Jude the Obscure,* the unresolved struggle for reader identification in *The Return of the Native.* In particular, the choice of method accounts for the failure of *Far from the Madding Crowd* to rise above the polyphony of irony.

Hardy in each novel uses a dominant aesthetic feature, or organizing principle, that informs the entire work and creates the peculiar quality of tragedy that distinguishes it: the arrangement of opposing qualities in *Far from the Madding Crowd;* the conflict of value-systems in *The Return of the Native;* the incorporation of a view of history that shapes plot and characterization in *The Mayor of Casterbridge;* the indirect expression of tragic significance through a conflation of characterizations in *The Woodlanders;* the intensity that directs the characters' behavior in much the same way that it guides the readers' reaction in *Tess of the d'Urbervilles;* and the manipulation of perspective that evaluates the protagonist in *Jude the Obscure* without confusing the narrator's personality for the author's. These various devices of Hardy's are manifest in the very nature of the novels, offering restrictions on and opportunities for the expression of certain kinds of emotions and themes. Hardy never repeated a dominant organizing technique, though he might use the technique again in a subordinate role; for example, the pattern of opposition that supports the theme in *Far from the Madding Crowd* reappears in later novels, especially in *The Return of the Native* and *Jude the Obscure.*

The forms Hardy uses indicate marked growth in his ability to direct reader attention to the crucial tensions in his novels. The direction of his development is not unusual — from an early stiffness and artificiality of concept evolve subtlety of concept and flexibility in utilization — but it is the extent of the development that is noteworthy. By the end of his career as a novelist he incorporates elements of historical theory and mysticism into a lexical and syntactic matrix that has changed but slightly since his earliest writing.

His early novels contain obvious formal devices and are structured in a very strained fashion. The manner in which these novels are made to fit restrictive criteria—for instance, the 2-3-4-3-2 progression of character relationships in *Far from the Madding Crowd*—makes them, in large part, exercises in self-apprenticeship. That after *Far from the Madding Crowd* and *The Return of the Native* he deliberately wrote his next novels in totally different manners (especially notable is his rejection, after the success of *Far from the Madding Crowd,* of the idea of a "woodlands story") reinforces the image of Hardy as autodidact, consciously putting himself to particular, and foreign, tasks. He gained genuine success—both artistically and financially—only after he realized that Wessex provided all the variety of dilemma, mood, and social levels that he had been searching for in other milieus.

Beginning with *The Mayor of Casterbridge,* the forms of Hardy's novels became increasingly free of mechanical impositions. The reason perhaps is that he had become confident enough of his artistic resources—in addition to his acceptance that his true subject was tragedy in a rural setting—to base his organization on general schemes or even abstractions rather than on mechanical patterns such as dichotomy and contrast. The scheme he employed in *The Mayor of Casterbridge* combines Aristotle's dictum of stature within a society, Auguste Comte's idea of cyclic change, and his own variation upon the idea of cycle that makes key events in the novel commentaries upon the completed action. Hardy's utilization of these *données* in *The Mayor of Casterbridge* does not limit his imaginative perceptions of the situation and the characters that embody the forms. Thus Henchard, unlike Clym and Eustacia, has an existence independent of the novel's forms. He lives his life within a cycle, he is aware of the cycle—his awareness even accounts, in part, for his death—but the range of employment of the cycle in *The Mayor of Casterbridge* has an enriching effect quite unlike the idea of conflicting temporal existences in *The Return of the Native,* in which every point of relation between the two protagonists is twisted into a polemic.

One can only conjecture Hardy's reasons, conscious or unconscious, for adopting relatively unrestricting forms in the novels that follow *The Mayor of Casterbridge* (except *The Well-Beloved*). These forms fit in with Hardy's intuitive development of initial situations, just as, inversely, the restraining effect implicit in the formal principles in the early novels would seem to be in accord with a desire for imposed limitations upon the imagination natural in the early plans of a deliberate and self-trained writer.

The formal basis of the last three great novels is open-ended in that no specific demands are made in terms of interrelations of components or interlocking patterns of significance, in contrast to the closed systems of *Far from the Madding Crowd* and *The Return of the Native.* To say that the later novels are open-ended in their formal bases is not to suggest that the forms of these novels are chaotic. The structure of *The Woodlanders* evolves from a concept of local heroism and tragic significance that gives point to its wide range of human types; *Tess of the d'Urbervilles* is a justification of the central role of the protagonist's consciousness; and the difficulty of accepting the perspective of the narrator or of any character imposes upon *Jude the Obscure* a relativism that the plot fulfills.

It is through Hardy's designs, and through the control they exercise upon the novels, that his concepts of tragedy acquire vitality and specialness. The tragic characters possess intensity and self-awareness; their experiences have a universality. Large questions are posed about man's relationship with the universe he must live in and with the other humans who in personal and social relations constitute his ties to humanity; those questions are explored with responsibility, because choices in Hardy stem from characters' inner selves, and bear consequences. In the narrative, tragic vision is focused upon a closely knit series of events, usually occurring in a Wessex scene with qualities of a microcosm, and the vision is maintained through the control of authorial distance and point of view. These characteristics that make up tragedy for Hardy are conventional when stated boldly without attempting to distinguish shadings. But when they operate within his linguistic framework of yoked naturalness and elaborateness and within his direct and piercing portrayal of the suffering that man causes other men and himself, they help to create the most substantial tragic world which is to be found in English literature during the last hundred years.

# 2

## FAR FROM THE MADDING CROWD:

### *The Non-Tragic Predecessor*

The critical reputation of *Far from the Madding Crowd* has remained the most stable among Hardy's novels, and for good reason. Few issues tantalize and puzzle its readers. The first installment in *Cornhill Magazine* showed that it would be a powerful novel. Published anonymously as a serial, it at first provoked speculation that George Eliot was the author,[1] but Hardy's grammatical and syntactic infelicities were soon compared unfavorably with her skill.[2] All in all, the immediate critical response was warm, despite qualifications, and the novel has continued to hold a high place among the Wessex novels. It became the standard against which the rest were evaluated, and remained so throughout Hardy's career. That the others were usually thought inferior is more an index to critical predisposition than to the final superiority of *Far from the Madding Crowd;* but that it could be consistently used for a model indicates that its solid merits were recognized. The novel is still widely praised for its rustic characters, its dramatic scenes, its closely detailed, accurate, and, more importantly, evocative depictions of sheep-raising, and its correlations between man's repetitious but sometimes frenzied activities and the calmly implacable but sometimes ferocious forces of nature.

*Far from the Madding Crowd* is incidentally but crucially at the heart of this study which emphasizes Hardy's use of a variety of formal methods to express tragedy. Its principal technical feature works against tragic expression, although Hardy indicates an awareness of the possibility of turning the novel into a tragic fiction. Moreover, the technique he employs here — schematism and dichotomy — is congenial to an initial exploration of many themes he later developed. Thus, these aspects of the techniques of *Far from the Madding Crowd* are pertinent to a full understanding of Hardy's methods and ideas; the greater subtlety of the later novels blurs the edges of a vision of life composed of dynamically contrasting forces which Hardy expresses in *Far from the Madding Crowd.* The late nineteenth- and early twentieth-century interpretation of Hardy's novels as architectural constructions is not inaccurate; but critics and early readers of Hardy failed to observe his efforts to subordinate his instinctive "architectural vision" to humane studies of emotion and thought which through his skill he was able to develop over the years. Thus, although his last novel, *Jude the Obscure,* is built on the idea of contrasts, as Hardy admitted,[3] it possesses greater passion and understanding than *Far from the Madding Crowd,* in which the contrasts are organizational devices for plot and character presentation and never become dramatic interplays of personality and philosophical viewpoints. We also see in *Far from the Madding Crowd* the degree to which this architectural patterning is innate to Hardy, in the balance of sentence structures and antithetical contents of his sentences. The architectural filigree is an integral device for communicating Hardy's vision of the world and for indicating the interpretive limits of the novel.

That *Far from the Madding Crowd* is the most rigidly conceived and schematically executed of Hardy's novels is a critical cliché. The symmetry of the overall plot is nearly perfect, according to James Wright:

> At the beginning, we see the shepherd Oak wooing Bathsheba. Shortly after his failure he begins to blend with the landscape in his silent devotion to the heroine. Then Bathsheba more or less promises herself to Boldwood. Just as she is to accept Boldwood's offer of engagement, she becomes infatuated with Sergeant Troy. Boldwood joins Oak in a hopeless patience. Shortly after Bathsheba's marriage to Troy, she begins her descent. She learns that he is a cad, and marriage seems hell to her.

After the incident of Fanny Robin's death, Troy vanishes. Boldwood
emerges from the background to woo Bathsheba again. Troy returns,
and is killed. Boldwood is imprisoned. At last, Bathsheba and Oak are
together, as they were at the beginning. We might schematize the action according to the number of wooers surrounding Bathsheba as the
novel progresses: 2-3-4-3-2. [4]

Wright comments that although "the scheme is charmingly neat . . .
it is also satanically false to Hardy" in that it bypasses Hardy's embodi-
ment of his vision in a rich context of knowledge of nature. The
scheme may indeed be satanically false in this respect, but its charming neatness is supplemented by being aesthetically true, for this
novel contains a number of dichotomizing elements that parallel the
sharp outlines of plot as Wright sketches it and that lead us, in this
early Hardy novel, straight into the essential quality of his vision and
of his "message" concerning human life.

In passages of both description and analysis in *Far from the
Madding Crowd*, Hardy uses contrasting terms and details to convey
shades of meaning. Hardy's intention would appear to be the attainment of precision and denotativeness, although the matters dealt with
are connotative or evaluative. Instead of giving the effect of a balanced consideration of the issues, Hardy's mannerism creates a sense
of rigidity and limits imaginative identification. Isolating the elements in a human quality, or indicating the extremes of a manner, or
ascribing general meaning to an individual act — all these practices,
which are pronounced aspects of the style of *Far from the Madding
Crowd*, create a schism between the conception Hardy presumably
has and its realization or rendering. With equal cause, a reader's
reaction to this technique could be to recognize it either as a grotesque turning of human subtleties into mechanical variations or as
a writer's effort to overcome the fuzziness of his idea as to what he
actually wants to make of his materials. Some examples of Hardy's
schematic style in this novel are: when Oak first sees Bathsheba she
is thinking about her "face and form"; Oak thinks that "the self-con-
sciousness shown would have been vanity if a little more pronounced,
dignity if a little less" (p. 20). When Bathsheba leaves, the infatuated
Oak returns to his work "with an air between that of Tragedy and
Comedy" (p. 21). Preparing to propose to Bathsheba, Oak makes "a
toilet of a nicely-adjusted kind — of a nature between the carefully

neat and carelessly ornate — of a degree between fine-market-day and wet-Sunday selection" (p. 28). After describing the illusion that the clouds, snow, and surfaces outside Troy's barracks resemble a cavern, Hardy notes: "We turn our attention to the left-hand [that is, abstract] characteristics; which were flatness in respect of the river, verticality in respect of the wall behind it, and darkness as to both. These features made up the mass. If anything could be darker than the sky, it was the wall, and if anything could be gloomier than the wall it was the river beneath" (p. 96). Another example of this quality of Hardy's style is his description of Bathsheba's reading the Book of Ruth to learn whom she is to marry: "It was Wisdom in the abstract facing Folly in the concrete" (p. 108). Finally, Boldwood in entering the malthouse bestows upon each man already there "a nod of a quality between friendliness and condescension" (p. 125).

The variety of the quotations makes evident that Hardy employs this technique in nearly every facet of the novel — characterization, plot, philosophizing, setting. The quotations are obviously dichoto-mous in their division of features of human life into categories. The book abounds with other, less clear instances of schematism. For example, Hardy comments about Oak's early love for the youthful and vivacious Bathsheba, "Love is a possible strength in an actual weakness. Marriage transforms a distraction into a support, the power of which should be, and happily often is, in direct proportion to the degree of imbecility it supplants" (p. 27). Mark Clark is "a genial and pleasant gentleman, whom to meet anywhere in your travels was to know, to know was to drink with, and to drink with was, unfortunately, to pay for" (p. 62). In describing the night when Fanny arrives at Troy's barracks to remind him that he had promised to marry her, Hardy employs a range of potential reactions to the moment: "It was a night when sorrow may come to the brightest without causing any great sense of incongruity: when, with impressible persons, love be-comes solicitousness, hope sinks to misgiving, and faith to hope: when the exercise of memory does not stir feelings of regret at opportuni-ties for ambition that have been passed by, and anticipation does not prompt to enterprise" (p. 95). Again, "the whole effect" of a certain sunrise "resembled a sunset as childhood resembles age" (p. 114).

These examples are clearly written, but the same technique is employed with Hardy's strained erudition and gnarled phraseology which have brought groans of exasperation for a full century. An example from the first description of Gabriel will illustrate:

> On Sundays he was a man of misty views, rather given to postponing, and hampered by his best clothes and umbrella: upon the whole, one who felt himself to occupy morally that vast middle space of Laodicean neutrality which lay between the Communion people of the parish and the drunken section. [P. 1]

Even the explanation that follows immediately, "that is, he went to church, but yawned privately by the time the congregation reached the Nicene creed," is more of a self-ironic comment on the phraseology than it is a clarification of it.

# I

The total effect of Hardy's technique has not gone unnoticed by critics, although it has not been discussed at length.[5] Since Hardy's artistry is developmental rather than static, the technique is not used again in such a completely artificial fashion. Although he never became a fine stylist, he improved. As he proceeds to different aspects of his major themes in each novel, the methods he uses to convey the themes are appropriately altered also. His manner is direct in *Far from the Madding Crowd*, and not unexpectedly we find revelations here of Hardy's 1874 concepts of the themes he later made peculiarly his own, such as his ideas about tragedy, free will, and time.

Clearly, the schematic style has great effect upon the characterizations. Each major character has at least one set of opposing qualities. Oak, conveniently enough for his happiness, has arrived at the age of twenty-eight knowing his intellect and emotions are separated, a state of self-awareness that keeps him from being either an impulsive youth or a prejudiced family man (p. 3), and allowing him to weather utter financial ruin with only a modicum of despair and even to attain a more dignified calm in the process (pp. 41, 44). The description of Gabriel's personal appearance uses contrasting extremes to indicate his ordinariness in Bathsheba's eyes:

Gabriel's features adhered throughout their form so exactly to the middle line between the beauty of St. John and the ugliness of Judas Iscar-
iot, as represented in a window of the church he attended, that not a
single lineament could be selected and called worthy either of distinction or notoriety. The red-jacketed and dark-haired maiden seemed to
think so too, for she carelessly glanced over him, and told her man to
drive on. [P. 6]

Hardy's penchant for creating character out of opposing qualities occasionally results in a wooden being. Indeed, the first description of Şergeant Troy in chapter 25 presents him as possessing contradictions, modifications, and opposites beyond which he almost
never develops. His attitude toward time obliterates the past and
stunts the future, leaving him shriveled in the present (p. 190); he
seems to have immense capacities for pleasure because he has no
moral sense of the threat of experience, but actually he has less than
more serious-minded people have (p. 191); his reason and his propen-
sities do not influence each other (p. 191); his vices are spruce rather
than ugly (p. 191). Though he is full of energy, "his activities were less
of a locomotive than a vegetative nature" (p. 191), by which Hardy
seems to mean that Troy is indifferent about the area of his activities
—"they were exercised on whatever object chance might place in
their way." Troy even carries on personal relationships in terms of
contradictory absolutes: "in dealing with womankind the only alternative to flattery was cursing and swearing. There was no third
method. 'Treat them fairly, and you are a lost man,' he would say"
(p. 193). The initial expectations set up in chapter 25 are fulfilled in
the remainder of the novel, when Troy slips abruptly from aimless
flattery to honest admiration of Bathsheba (pp. 202-03); when he stops
loving her abruptly after marriage (p. 299) and comes again to prefer
Fanny (cruelly telling Bathsheba so after Fanny's death [p. 345] );
when he is easily discouraged from reforming by the "accidental"
action of a waterspout (pp. 364-65); when he goes indifferently for a
swim and seizes the existence of a strong current to have it thought he
had drowned; and finally when he returns from his wanderings lusting
almost as much for Bathsheba's wealth as for her person (pp. 416,
421). Since Troy's character throughout has no subtle features, the
reader shifts aimlessly from bemused acquiescence in his audacity to

disgust at his rootlessness, but never gives Troy the sympathy that he offers to Boldwood. Troy's failure to attract sympathy can, I think, be attributed to Hardy's method of characterization. Always suspended between alternatives of mood or attitude, Troy never presents himself as *being*; and because his alternative patterns are not developmental, he never presents himself as *becoming*. In effect, then, Troy is characterized by a sequence of vignettes held together by his relationships with other characters rather than by any unity within himself.

Boldwood, too, is a stiff figure; but he is more consistent within the context of the novel because the alternatives which divide his energies more closely resemble the dichotomous qualities in other characters, and because they suggest a personality created by experiences more profound and painful than any in Troy's life. Boldwood seems to have a symmetrical existence (p. 112), though it is actually a symmetry composed of "enormous antagonistic forces" presently held in "perfect balance" (p. 137). Suitably, the dichotomous elements in Boldwood's make-up are absolute indifference and self-indulgence: "His equilibrium disturbed, he was in extremity at once. If an emotion possessed him at all, it ruled him; a feeling not mastering him was entirely latent" (p. 137). He says at one point that he prefers his present misery of being in love to his former "ignorant and cold darkness" (p. 231), an indication that for Boldwood a moderate middle position is not possible. A completely serious man, "he had no light and careless touches in his constitution, either for good or for evil" (p. 137). Once having devoted himself to the sender of the valentine even before he knows who had sent it, Boldwood's absorption with Bathsheba and his increasing frenzy during the evolution of the situation — through Bathsheba's rejection of his proposal, her marriage to Troy, her "widowhood," and her final reluctant agreement to reward his suffering and constancy — are inevitable. The essential unity of Boldwood's nature, his own awareness of the extremities he allows himself to go to (p. 261) counter the disparate and aimless but headlong rush of Troy toward their mutual destruction. Self-control marks the early Boldwood; its decay traces the effects of a contradictory, frustrated impulse upon a distracted extremist personality. Fearing Bathsheba may be lured into loving Troy, he is conscious that he has lost the dignity and firmness of his old self (p. 261); but notwithstanding, he does not hesitate to show himself ethically inferior to Troy. He tries to bribe Troy to marry Fanny, and he readily accepts the idea that Troy has brought Bathsheba to dishonor when he hears her invite him into her house (pp. 263-67). His grief at the loss of Bathsheba makes him indifferent whether or not his grain ricks are protected from rain (p. 294), an abandonment of worldly responsibilities whose culpability is suggested by the firm acceptance of the importance of material realities by Oak. Once the disequilibrium is formed in Boldwood's personality, it can never be dislodged, not even, perhaps, if Bathsheba had ultimately married him. His equilibrium may have been unsettled before the time of the novel, for there are "old floodmarks faintly visible" that reveal his "wild capabilities." But precisely because the reader has never seen him at "the high tides which caused them" (p. 138), he cannot believe Boldwood has the capacity to reestablish the stolidity and calm of his initial appearance in the novel.

It is, however, in the characterization of Bathsheba that the dichotomy of Hardy's style has full power, and here it is effectively modified by the vital individuality of the character. Despite the masculine agricultural interests that dominate the novel, Bathsheba is the unifying element. She alone develops new facets to her character over the course of the action; Boldwood and Troy may evince what appear to the other characters to be new traits, but the traits are implicit in the author's initial presentation. Oak, it is true, also develops, but very early in the novel (p. 44), and only through authorial pronouncement — his behavior before the loss of his sheep does not indicate he had ever seriously *lacked* dignity, the "new" characteristic he acquires. Bathsheba, on the other hand, definitely evolves from a flirtatious, light-hearted girl to a self-confident farmer, to a chastened but stubborn wife, to a tormented woman wanting only peace, to a subdued female anxious for the protective strength of a Gabriel Oak.

The terms of dichotomy that distinguish Bathsheba's character are initially similar to those used to characterize Oak — intellect and emotion. On Bathsheba's first appearance, looking at herself (surreptitiously) in a mirror, the terms to describe her might be vanity and a consciousness that vanity is not admirable; on her second appearance, riding a horse astraddle instead of sidesaddle and lying flat on her horse's back to pass under a low branch, the terms might be practicality and awareness of propriety (pp. 4-7, 17-21). At this early stage of the novel, the division in Bathsheba's character bears largely upon her attractiveness for Oak and upon the wisdom of an ambitious sheep farmer marrying a girl whose habits of mind are not yet fixed. But the issues rapidly become more complex and morally significant. Following Boldwood's first proposal, Hardy-as-narrator analyzes Bathsheba's character in an expository section (pp. 148-49). Bathsheba is a woman who appeals to her "understanding" for deliverance from her "whims," terms that clearly parallel "intellect" and "emotion." An example of Hardy's dichotomous phraseology is the following:

> Bathsheba's was an *impulsive* nature under a *deliberative* aspect. An *Elizabeth in brain* and a *Mary Stuart in spirit,* she often performed actions of the *greatest temerity* with a manner of *extreme discretion.* Many of her thoughts were perfect *syllogisms*; unluckily they always remained thoughts. Only a few were *irrational assumptions*; but, unfortunately, they were the ones which most frequently grew into deeds. [P. 149; my italics]

By indicating that Bathsheba in her uneducated state allows irrationality to dominate her rationality in situations leading to action, Hardy prepares the ground for her to learn a facet of life that constitutes a major theme in his fiction: the necessity to control the impulses which put one in opposition to the forces of the universe. He also prepares us for Bathsheba's great error in her personal relationships. Since she has no "whim" for the "married state in the abstract" and no emotion toward Boldwood, she has no trouble in behaving correctly toward him. Indeed, she nearly allows herself to marry him, an act bereft of passion but buttressed by months of deliberation. But Troy, unlike Boldwood or Oak, *does* create, or at least awaken, impulses in Bathsheba that reenforce the sense of her unreliability in matters of emotion. Throughout the novel Bathsheba seems torn between the unconscious desire to be sexually mastered and the desire to maintain sexual independence and even to exert sexual authority. Hardy says that "Bathsheba loved Troy in the way that only self-reliant women love when they abandon their self-reliance" (p. 214); and even more clearly dichotomous is his remark that Bathsheba "felt her *impulses* to be pleasanter guides than her *discretion*" (p. 215; my italics).

Bathsheba's abandonment of self-reliance and discretion repeats the action of her father toward the problem of fidelity to her mother. Her father's "will" had been chaste, but his "heart" had wandered (pp. 69-70), a problem that was solved (humorously) only when Mrs. Everdene was induced to take off her wedding ring and thus prevent her husband from giving "his eyes to unlawfulness entirely," as Joseph Poorgrass puts in. This indication of a dichotomy that is in Bathsheba's blood, so to speak, emphasizes the depth of her task in reconciling the two aspects of her personality, and suggests further the structural balance achieved in the novel through Oak's mastery over opposing qualities that are similar to those that war within Bathsheba. The suggestion, explicitly, is that Bathsheba requires an *external* control of her impulses, a control that Oak provides by example and, at the end of the novel, by his marriage to her.

Hardy's analysis of Bathsheba after the sword-exercise display by Troy (a heated scene that is replete with sexual connotations[6] ) explains Bathsheba's discordant qualities at the height of their manifestation. Though she is a "woman of the world," it is a world of rural verities. "Her love was entire as a child's, and though warm as summer it was fresh as spring. Her culpability lay in her making no attempt to control feeling by subtle and careful inquiry into consequences"; even the "folly" of falling in love as she does is "almost foreign to her intrinsic nature" (pp. 214-15). The complexity of personality which this analysis implies — especially the abandonment that Bathsheba feels toward Troy, and her feeling that impulse is more pleasant than discretion where Troy is concerned — goes far to justify the peculiar rationale with which Bathsheba pursues Troy to Bath: she goes to see him in order to renounce him (and thus save his life from Boldwood's jealous fury) (p. 247). Once there, of course, she is easy prey to his threat to love someone else if she will not marry him. Troy obviously understands Bathsheba's subconscious motives better than she does.

The middle portion of the novel presents a Bathsheba who is between two primary stages of her development. (In the sense of being a personality evolving in definable progression she indicates another aspect of Hardy's schematic style.) As Troy remarks shortly after their marriage, Bathsheba has lost her "pluck and sauciness" (p. 299); as Hardy remarks after Fanny's death and the confrontation with Troy, Bathsheba has lost the "vitality of youth in her without substituting the philosophy of maturer years" (p. 367). She does not remain in this awkward stasis. She becomes more charming to the "middle-aged" Boldwood because "her exuberance of spirit was pruned down; the original phantom of delight had shown herself to be not too bright for human nature's daily food, and she had been able to enter this second poetical phase without losing much of the first in the process" (p. 382), a syntactically complex way of suggesting that Bathsheba if left alone would be able to adjust herself to widowhood. She is not, of course, left alone; and after being forced by Boldwood to come to a decision, she remains hidden behind a mask of inability to feel. Finally, almost totally subdued and dependent on Oak, she enters into a mature recognition of the limitations and blessings of unambitious existence.

# II

The presentation of Bathsheba particularly, then, makes decipherable the purpose of Hardy's schematic style, showing how thoroughly this technique dominates the expression of values in the novel. We begin to see how such a style can benefit a book like *Far from the Madding Crowd,* which presents Hardy's first full effort to unite the abstract themes that are characteristic of his great novels. In tracing Bathsheba's development from one extreme of the impulse-discretion continuum to the other, Hardy suggests that the ideal state is not one of perfect balance, as for instance, it is implicitly in Jane Austen. Oak, the moral touchstone, keeps his impulse always supremely controlled; he subdues his personal feelings because he senses that the universe is a mighty and potentially destructive force. The peasants, the moral base of the society, generally accept the conditions of their lot, and when they "rebel," or give way to impulse, as Joseph Poorgrass does in stopping for drinks while bringing Fanny's body home for burial, they are brought up sharply. Hardy's emotional allegiance may be with the strugglers, but his vision of the universe urges upon him the awareness that exertions of ego or desire bring on chastisement and suffering. He who attempts to override universal forces (including those portrayed in social bodies and laws) is made to realize the cost of self-expression and self-indulgence.

The contradiction that is inherent between Hardy's idea of man's correct posture toward nature's overbearing force and his sympathy for those who do not or cannot maintain that posture sets up in *Far from the Madding Crowd* a pattern of dichotomies that continue to engross Hardy in later novels.

Man in Hardy's works is an alien element within the cosmos. A sentient being, he gains no special attention from the forces that are unconscious and therefore supremely indifferent to his hopes and efforts. The forces of the universe that oppose man do so partly in the form of chance and accident, such as the waterspout that despoils Fanny's grave after Troy has repentantly planted flowers there, partly in the uncontrollable demonstrations of raw might, such as the famous storm that threatens Bathsheba's stored crops and destroys Boldwood's. Those forces diminish the stature of man, revealing his comparative triviality and minuteness. As Gabriel and Bathsheba together watch a particularly spectacular flurry of lightning during the storm on the night of the harvest feast, Gabriel is thrilled by her presence and touch; "but love, life, everything human, seemed small and trifling in such close juxtaposition with an infuriated universe" (p. 287). Another scene of nature's danger to man is when Troy is swept out to sea on the current and in the distance sees Budmouth "quietly regarding his efforts" but indifferent to their success or failure (p. 370).

In *Far from the Madding Crowd,* one feature that sets off man from nature is that man projects his own mood onto natural scenes; the scenes possess in themselves only potentiality of interpretation. The small whirlpools in the river outside Troy's barracks make sounds "which a sad man would have called moans, and a happy man laughter" (p. 97). Bathsheba, frightened by Boldwood's threats against Troy, thinks of ways to warn Troy; she gazes at "indecisive and palpitating stars," notes "their silent throes amid the shades of peace" (p. 237), and regrets that she has no peace of her own. In man-created scenes, too, there is an artificial mood placed upon objects. As Troy waits amid the tittering old women for Fanny to come to their wedding, a church clock ticks. "One could almost be positive that there was a malicious leer upon the hideous creature's face, and a mischievous delight in its twitchings" (p. 131). Troy accepts the waterspout's destruction of the flowers as a sign that his effort at reform is being ridiculed:

> Troy's brow became heavily contracted. He set his teeth closely, and his compressed lips moved as those of one in great pain. This singular accident, by a strange confluence of emotions in him, was felt as the sharpest sting of all. . . . A man who has spent his primal strength in journeying in one direction has not much spirit left for reversing his course. Troy had, since yesterday, faintly reversed his; but the merest opposition had disheartened him. To turn about would have been hard enough under the greatest providential encouragement; but to find that Providence, far from helping him into a new course, or showing any wish that he might adopt one, actually jeered his first trembling and critical attempt in that kind, was more than nature could bear.
>
> He slowly withdrew from the grave. He did not attempt to fill up the hole, replace the flowers, or do anything at all. He simply threw up his cards and forswore his game for that time and always. |Pp. 363, 364-65|

The narrator's tone implies that Troy reads mockery into entirely coincidental events — but even the narrator refers to the "vengeance" that the spout directs animistically into Fanny's grave (p. 362).

The complexity of man's relationship with nature is also sharply delineated in the occurrences following Bathsheba's night spent in the thicket after she has fled from Troy. When she first awakens, she is refreshed and rejuvenated by the spontaneity of the chirping birds, the beauty of the sunrise. "Day was just dawning, and beside its cool air and colours her heated actions and resolves of the night stood out in lurid contrast" (p. 347). Another aspect of nature is made apparent to Bathsheba instantly; looking toward the east, "between the beautiful yellowing ferns" she sees a fungi-infested swamp, ugly and malignant, which "exhaled the essences of evil things in the earth" (pp. 347-48). Recognizing the malign aspect that nature can direct toward man, Bathsheba is made fearful "at the thought of having passed the night on the brink of so dismal a place" (p. 348). But seeing the two sides of the same situation does not exhaust the significance of this scene. Immediately after recognizing the evilness of the swamp, and still miserable about Troy and Fanny, Bathsheba is able to be "faintly amused" at a rustic boy's method of learning his psalter (p. 348). And the evil aspects of the swamp are disparaged by the servant girl Liddy, who walks across the swamp in her anxiety to assure herself that her mistress is all right after a night of sleeping in the open (p. 349). By relegating dangerous conditions in nature to a secondary place in day-to-day living, Liddy demonstrates the peasant's right to a stable existence. Liddy's act is a great deal like Oak's construction of a lightning rod during the great storm. Hardy's point is clear in both contexts. Man does have the possibility of free will and effective action in the face of what may seem to be a rancorous universe. Oak's knowing how to circumvent the dangers of lightning, and Liddy's selflessness and peasant's disinterest in challenging nature's authority, save them from destruction. But both *could* have been destroyed, a fate common to Hardy's later characters whose exercise of free will expresses rebellion against external power rather than acceptance of their own limited human abilities.

Hardy is also concerned with what he often called "the natural," which in *Far from the Madding Crowd* he presents through contrasts. What is natural is admirable to Hardy, what is unnatural is undesirable or destructive. Hardy uses the blazing Christmas engagement party Boldwood gives toward the end of the novel to make this point explicitly:

> Intended gaieties would insist upon appearing like solemn grandeurs, the organization of the whole effort was carried out coldly by hirelings, and a shadow seemed to move about the rooms, saying that the proceedings were unnatural to the place and the lone man who lived therein, and hence not good. [P. 412]

Even Boldwood's love for Bathsheba is judged adversely. His devotion does not stabilize his character, because it is based on misconceptions and inner imbalances. There is an ominous imagistic suggestion of Boldwood's inadequacies in a world where natural impulses are admired, in his first appearance as love smitten. After receiving the valentine and learning who had sent it, Boldwood cannot keep his eyes from Bathsheba at the next meeting of the Corn Market. But Bathsheba is not favorably impressed by his attention. "This was a triumph; and had it come naturally, such a triumph would have been the sweeter to her for this piquing delay. But it had been brought about by misdirected ingenuity, and she valued it only as she valued an artificial flower or a wax fruit" (p. 135). The psychological sources of unnaturalness in Boldwood are only hinted at by Hardy through Boldwood's almost delighted acquiescence to a six-year secret engagement to a woman who insists she cannot love him, and through his eager fetishistic accumulation of women's clothing of Bathsheba's size (pp. 442-43). He is not capable of Troy's forthright sexual purposiveness or of Oak's patient suppression of passion by means of physical activity and determined professional achievement.

In contrast to the distortions of Boldwood's personality, supposedly anchored but actually open to the gales, Bathsheba's whims are those of an inherent inconsistency natural in an inexperienced but generally kind girl.[7] And Oak's reliance upon tradition gives him a secure natural protection against both external threats to his well-being and internal temptations to his peace of mind — so secure, indeed, that Oak is never significantly tempted or threatened. That he does not become an uninteresting, wooden figure attests to Hardy's wisdom in placing Oak in a subordinate role in the plot while developing contrasts among the characters who surround him and in time provide him with a context in which to manifest his strength.

The idea of *natural* should not be equated with *nature* in a limited frame of reference, however. *Natural* is more than individual predispositions, basic drives, or behavior modeled on animal-like impercipience toward the future. Hardy does not forget that one facet of the externality which affects man's fate is society. That which is *natural*, then, might well be a special attribute of a society-oriented way of life, so long as that attribute provides a resource against life's incertitudes. This consideration explains a preference expressed by Oak toward two alternatives that superficially may seem equally unacceptable. When Bathsheba confides to him, fifteen months after Troy's disappearance at sea, that Boldwood is urging her to consent to a long engagement and that she thinks she must assent or Boldwood will go out of his mind, Oak evaluates the possible engagement in terms of heat and cold: "If wild heat had to do wi' it, making ye long to overcome the awkwardness about your husband's vanishing, it mid be wrong; but a cold-hearted agreement to oblige a man seems different, somehow" (p. 409). The advocacy of a "cold-hearted agreement to oblige a man" does not obviously typify Oak, nor does it immediately seem consistent with Hardy's usual attitude toward human relationships, while "wild heat" at least refers to an aspect of animal nature in humanity. That Oak prefers coldness to emotion as a guide to the conduct of personal relationships is a consistent manifestation of his principles, however. A cold-hearted agreement in this context becomes, in other contexts, a rational and businesslike approach on how to decide issues. For example, Oak's energetic efforts to protect the wheat and barley ricks during the storm are impelled primarily by materialistic and utilitarian considerations, albeit underlined by the thought that the ricks are the property of "the woman I have loved so dearly." He precisely calculates the value of the grain and sees the usefulness of grain in a deeper perspective: "Seven hundred and fifty pounds in the divinest form that money can wear — that of necessary food for man and beast: should the risk be run of deteriorating this bulk of corn to less than half its value, because of the instability of a woman?" (p. 279). Later, with the job of covering the ricks partly finished, the danger of lightning becomes more apparent. Again, his reflections are in materialistic terms: "Was his life so valuable to him after all? What were his prospects that he should be so chary of running risk, when important and urgent labour could not be carried on without such risk?" (p. 285). And finally, during the heavy rain he drives in spars randomly, covering "more and more safely from ruin this distracting impersonation of seven hundred pounds"(p. 292). For Oak, concern with agricultural husbandry is materialistic, and although such concern could be dignified by being called an abstract duty, Oak sees it as a matter of finance and produce. Even his love life shows a similar straightforward acceptance of financial necessities. After the collapse of his sheep-raising venture in chapter 5, he accepts as inevitable and natural that Bathsheba should ignore him as a possible object of love. To Oak, and to his society, to lose one's position is to lose something intrinsic in his relations with others. With the other farm workers, who had never had any position, Oak's ill fortune is a matter for commiseration and comment, but not for undue lamentation or affected pity. For Oak, then, and for his society, frank, non-avaricious materialism is natural; and his advocacy to Bathsheba of a cold-hearted engagement with Boldwood allows her a way of life that is compatible with both her personal reluctance and her public responsibleness. None of the heroes of Hardy's later novels is able to piece together a fabric that justifies according to a social standard the individual's self and his responsibilities; this indicates a cause — as well as an effect — of the collapse of the *détente* between society and the individual in Wessex. Those characters closest to Oak — Winterborne and Melbury in *The Woodlanders* — are unable to provide a balance between the opposing demands of society and of individualism. Indeed, Melbury's temporary alienation from principle deprives Giles of a context in which his selflessness can be fulfilled.

# III

*Far from the Madding Crowd* can generically be called *tragic* only by accepting Boldwood and Troy as protagonists and by defining tragedy in the broadest sense as education through suffering. Given the terms of our discussion, it is not immediately evident why this should be so: most modern theories of tragedy are based on the idea of dichotomy, balance, or dialectic. Nietzsche's description of the conflicting but balanced poles of Dionysian and Apollonian impulses is developed more recently by Richard Sewall and Murray Kreiger, although they prefer the concept of irresolvable tension to that of perfect balance. But at least two factors prevent the novel from being a tragedy. Its moral message of accommodation to universal forces forestalls the asking of ultimate questions; in Kreiger's terms, the "tragic vision" of which Oak is capable is overwhelmed by an "ethical vision" which keeps him in his place, earnestly striving toward humdrum, if healthy, goals. Equally to the point, the pervasiveness of the schematic style helps us to understand why the novel is not tragic. The aesthetic method of *Far from the Madding Crowd* is simply too stark, too rigidly antithetical, to create reader involvement or complexity of reaction. The assumption of the aesthetic in this novel is that any and all reactions to situations will be between two extremes, or on one of two extremes. Both the *alternatives* and the preferable *choice* are clearly indicated, preventing ambiguity and terror raised by unforseeable alternatives, and in effect obviating suspenseful allegiance to a beleaguered ideal whose ultimate value is in question.

Hardy continued to use the schematic method, but certainly the more direct and unmodified its use the less successful the novel. *The Return of the Native*, for instance, is permeated with this sense of dichotomy — primarily in the cleavage between the tragic connotations in the chapters "Queen of Night" and "'My Mind to Me a

Kingdom Is'" and the mundane persons of Eustacia and Clym, and in the descriptions of Eustacia and Clym as characters symbolic of world views. The effect of this early mannerism of Hardy is to atomize his characterizations in *The Return of the Native* well beyond the desiderata of tragedy. This device was consciously used by Hardy, but his style of tragedy was still evolving in *The Return of the Native*, and his use of dichotomy was only partially successful. *Jude the Obscure* demonstrates a successful employment of dichotomous structure which can be attributed to the greater complexity of personality discussed above, and to the broadness of the contrasts (see n.3). The dichotomies of *Jude the Obscure* are not expressed through the rhetoric of the sentence and paragraph as pervasively as they are in *Far from the Madding Crowd*.

The possibility of tragedy in a context where the individual will counts for very little is a major concern throughout Hardy's career; in *Far from the Madding Crowd* he initiates his expression of the central feature of tragedy in fiction, intensity of personality realization, coordinating this feature with other basic concepts. While the idea is developed much more subtly later, especially in *Tess of the d'Urbervilles*, Hardy's first approach is in the familiar dichotomous manner: he defines by setting qualities and characters against each other. It is pathetic little Fanny Robin who provides him with the opportunity to theorize, to indicate that tragedy cannot exist without strength in the individual character. As she struggles painfully toward the Casterbridge workhouse, Hardy notes her inability to soliloquize grandly: "Extremity of feeling lessens the individuality of the weak, as it increases that of the strong" (p. 305). The division according to potentiality between tragic and non-tragic persons is restated after Fanny's death, as Hardy directly compares the physical sufferings of Fanny and the psychological sufferings of Bathsheba when Troy kneels at Fanny's coffin to kiss the corpse of the girl he had spitefully refused to marry. "Capacity for intense feeling is proportionate to the general intensity of the nature, and perhaps in all Fanny's sufferings, much greater relatively to her strength, there never was a time when she suffered in an absolute sense what Bathsheba suffered now" (pp.343-44). Through this simple and perhaps unnecessarily obvious contrast, Hardy outlines what he considers the essential component of tragedy, the intensity of inner experience (rather than the breath of experience). At the outset of his career, then, Hardy does not adhere to the Aristotelian theory of tragedy based on an emphasis on plot and on the worldly position of his protagonist; his fondness for sensational plots cannot prevent us from seeing that his created beings are the basis of his popularity. The marvel is that he created so many individuals capable of intense suffering without repeating himself.[8]

Accompanying the dichotomous expression of tragic potentiality is the never-resolved dialectic concerning free will and determinism (or effects of circumstance); this dialectic is dealt with strikingly in *Far from the Madding Crowd*. Never in his career was Hardy able to settle the conflicting claims of philosophical determinism and seeming freedom in choice and act. *The Mayor of Casterbridge* is in part a brief for free will; *The Dynasts* presents explicit images of a mechanistic universe; but neither work excludes the opposing concept, and the well-known final passages of *The Dynasts* imply a meliorist view — which Hardy learned in part from Eduard von Hartmann — that as the universal Will becomes more conscious of its own workings, there will be greater opportunities for effective individual free will. Hardy's analysis of the responsibility for Boldwood's infatuation is one of his most complex grapplings with this conflict. Boldwood is absorbed in guessing at the motive of the sender of the valentine, mistakenly assuming that there must have been a motive. "It is foreign to a mystified condition of mind to realize of the mystifier that the processes of approving a course suggested by circumstance, and of striking out a course from inner impulse, would look the same in the result. The vast difference between starting a train of events, and directing into a particular groove a series already started, is rarely apparent to the person confounded by the issue" (p. 113). Boldwood's ignorance makes him think he is taking the latter course, the more deterministic one, but as the reader knows, Bathsheba did not intend to start a "chain of events." Hardy makes explicit their acting at cross-purposes: "Boldwood's blindness to the difference between approving of what circumstances suggest, and originating what they do not suggest, was well matched by Bathsheba's insensibility to the possibly great issues of little beginnings" (p. 134). Bathsheba, then, thinks she has the choice of making a consequence-less act, but her future is strongly determined by this act of purposeless free will. (The act is, however, described in such a way as to emphasize the accidental fea-

tures in the linking of events culminating in the sending of the valentine — especially the fortuitous existence of a seal that prints "Marry
Me," surely not a usual item on farmers' writing desks [see pp. 110-
11].) Boldwood, on the other hand, thinks he is affecting a chain of
events he did not initiate, but actually he provides the impetus for all
that follows. The point of these expository sections in the novel is
that what *seems* to be an act of free will is not; conversely, what seems
to have been determined by a force external to the individual is
actually initiated by that individual. The implication of the dichotomy
is clear: human vision is too limited, its perspective too egoistic, for
the absolute truth of the quality of man's freedom to be ever securely
known by the individual, and, by extension, by the race of man. The
irony of the situation revealed by the valentine incident spills over
into the rest of the book, until finally Bathsheba thinks that she is
being "coerced by a force [Boldwood] stronger than her own will"
(p. 407), not only to promise to enter into a six years' engagement
but also to fancy that she ought to promise. Bathsheba's direction-
lessness act of free will has led her into a situation permitting no
honorable alternatives. Fortunately for her own sense of integrity, not
to mention her happiness, Boldwood is caught in the chain of events
consequent upon his own unintentional act of free will. His murder of
Troy frees Bathsheba and, ironically, gives her back a measure of
freedom of choice.

Another dichotomous theme applicable to both Hardy's entire
body of work and his idea of tragedy is that of time. In *Far from the
Madding Crowd*, time is used to contrast two ways of life, the timeless
and permanent life of Weatherbury agriculture, and the exceedingly
temporal and transient life of Troy and, as the novel develops, of
Boldwood, both of whom are so involved in the frenzy of immediate
activity that they cannot adjust to another time pattern. Weatherbury
time is developed through the existence of the shearing barn, as old as
the village church, but unlike the church still used for the purpose
for which it was originally built and still a benefit to mankind (p. 165).
The descriptions of recurring rural activities throughout the book
also reflect upon the timeless quality of Weatherbury life. And of
course the coexistence of five generations of Smallburys demonstrates an indifference to age differentials among peasant stock that
is closely allied to their "Oriental indifference to the flight of time."

Opposed to this sense of immanent continuity is Sergeant Troy, to whom "memories were an encumbrance, and anticipations a superfluity," a man who cared "for what was before his eyes," who "was vulnerable only in the present....With him the past was yesterday; the future, to-morrow; never, the day after" (p. 190). Troy wants to have Bathsheba's traditionally furnished farmhouse redecorated, because in the old house he feels "like new wine in an old bottle" (p. 271). Boldwood cannot adjust his psychological time-sense after Troy's disappearance; he cruelly bullies Bathsheba into a lengthy engagement. Further, he betrays his disavowal of tradition when he asks Oak whether there is "any [necktie] knot in fashion" before his Christmas party (p. 414) — an act consistent with his "unnatural" behavior in planning such a party. In a limited respect, the peasants and Troy look at time similarly. The lives of both pass as an instant. The difference, however, is essential and obvious: the "instant" of the peasants' lives is centuries in length; their lives are an instant because they do not distinguish themselves apart from their forefathers and progeny (p. 463); they do not even distinguish historical from artistic events (p. 396). Troy's life is an instant, on the other hand, because its sensations are short in duration, usually failing to survive the immediate event he is participating in. Theoretically, perhaps, either time-sense can be employed in a narrative seeking to express the tragic. Yet clearly for the formulation of Hardy's own tragic sense, the peasants' view of time is paramount. It establishes an aura of permanence — in values, in personality traits, in social customs. It is against this aura that new traditions are evaluated and that protagonists struggle, trying to change or to exploit the "permanent" conditions of life. This struggle on the stage of time is most formative for the tragic plots of *The Return of the Native* and *The Mayor of Casterbridge*, but each of Hardy's novels relies on contrast in time-senses for an important share of its characterizations and effects.

# IV

Although Hardy works out some basic concepts of the mode within the story, *Far from the Madding Crowd* is not a tragedy. In addition to the effect of the schematic style, the novel does not achieve the power of tragedy because — unlike almost all of Hardy's creative expressions that approach tragic power — it possesses a resolution that awards happiness to the hero and heroine. It does so without the irony that makes Fancy Day's marriage to Dick Dewy in *Under the Greenwood Tree* a delightfully human sustainment of conflicting desires. Oak marries the mistress he has faithfully served for so long; and there is little doubt that Hardy intends the reader to understand Oak is being rewarded for his patience and his resignation, for his subservience to what Hardy later in life called the Immanent Will, and which in 1874 went by the name of circumstance. This denouement makes *Far from the Madding Crowd* the most positive in outlook of Hardy's novels, and along with its portrayal of a healthy and self-confident society it has become through the denouement a kind of touchstone for the other Wessex novels in the minds of contemporary reviewers and novel readers.

Literary critics generally are skeptical about the plausibility of happy endings in novels, but in *Far from the Madding Crowd* the ending is implicit in the novel's presuppositions about the relationship between struggle and punishment, acquiescence and contentment. The ending is true to its conditions and context; but there are certain modifying aspects of the denouement that critics have not overlooked. They note the peasants' anticipations of future strife in the marriage of Oak and Bathsheba, and the speed with which "the author disposes . . . of the rest of his story" after Troy's death.[9] Richard Carpenter thinks the ending is "a questionable sop to our feelings," and suggests that "the novel does not really end 'happily'" because "the vibrant and proud girl we see at the beginning has been as thoroughly destroyed as Troy and Boldwood."[10] I am not persuaded that these opinions are valid. It is true that the peasants josh Oak on the evening of his marriage because he can say "my wife" without a chill note in his voice, and that Jan Coggan adds, "twirling his eye, . . .'That improvement will come wi' time'" (p. 463). But Bathsheba and Oak have been too thoroughly tested and have come through too successfully for these remarks to carry much foreboding. As Joseph Poorgrass says with a "cheerful sigh" to close the novel, "But since 'tis as 'tis, why, it might have been worse, and I feel my thanks accordingly" (p. 464). Oak receives precisely the kind of happiness he would

choose: an unexciting filling of the general "void within him" that had
led to his first falling in love with Bathsheba (p. 16).

But the ending of *Far from the Madding Crowd* does have a
false quality about it, an internal belittlement of the sense of the natural shaping of personality through experience that the major part of
the novel portrays. This falseness results, I think, from Hardy's reluctance to compromise the suspense of the plot action leading to the
climax of Boldwood's frantic and desperate shooting of Troy. In order
to create the kind of tension necessary to justify aesthetically Boldwood's violence, the plot lines must be direct and the characterizations straightforward. It must seem as if the resolution of Bathsheba's
fate lies of necessity somewhere between the contradictory juris-
dictions of Boldwood, the imperious and dogged suitor, and Troy, the
imperious and egoistic husband, neither of whom has any com-
punctions in forcing Bathsheba into sexual or financial situations
against her will. Her will, of course, by this time favors peace; she says
she no longer has feeling or emotion (p. 418); she wants merely to be
left alone by Boldwood and to remain deserted by Troy. To have
allowed Oak a position in this Hardyan variant upon the *ménage à
trois* would have destroyed the suspense and the dichotomous style
that sustains it, for if Hardy had offered the suggestion that Bathsheba
had matured to the point of being able to accept Oak romantically
before her husband and Boldwood are removed from the competition,
there would have been less tension in the preparation for the violent
resolution of Troy's and Boldwood's pursuit of Bathsheba. The reader
would have had in his mind a confidence — or at least a distracting
suspicion — that Bathsheba would simply turn to Oak at the proper
time. The reader may have such a suspicion, nonetheless, but it is not
through direct authorial guidance.[11]

Even with these difficulties of emphasis, it is conceivable that
Hardy could have satisfactorily carried off the ultimate union of Oak
and Bathsheba had he truly felt the union was inevitable. But the
strain in fulfilling reader expectation is indicated by the sudden
sinking of the novel's tone through conventional patterns of coyness
and flirtatiousness, much as happens in the similar and more noto-
rious situation where Hardy's personal inclination and novelistic convention differed — book 6 of *The Return of the Native* with its coy
courtship of Diggory Venn and Thomasin. Even though Hardy's

inclination is evidently to reward Oak with Bathsheba's hand and her rented lands—that is, in *Far from the Madding Crowd* Hardy's inclination and novelistic convention are the same—his inclination does not inspire his imagination. Oak is prevented by an old oath (p. 36) from proposing to Bathsheba again—presumably the justification for having Bathsheba initiate the courtship leading to their marriage. The best device Hardy can muster to bring Bathsheba to the point of declaring her desire to marry Oak is Oak's statement during the winter that he intends to emigrate to California, an intention he drops immediately upon Bathsheba's expression of regret. He neglects to inform her of his change in plans, and three months pass with no further communication between the two about Oak's supposed departure. Bathsheba becomes more and more eager to have Oak remain in Weatherbury; Oak makes arrangements to take over another farm, again without telling Bathsheba. When Bathsheba makes her "climactic" visit to Oak's house at night to beg him to alter his plans of emigration, then, it is a purposeless errand. She thereupon falls into coquettishness as she had done in the early scenes when she forces Oak to admit his love for her, distorting her novel-long development toward sobriety and chastisement. Her laugh, "It seems exactly as if I had come courting you—how dreadful!" (p. 456), may make explicit Oak's reward for constancy, but it also stresses the comic conception of the reward system that Hardy is employing. Hardy implies that Bathsheba's previous disdain of Oak can be compensated for only by total subservience and by a turnabout of the sexual roles in the courtship which mocks Bathsheba's earlier efforts to usurp masculine prerogatives. This insertion of the comedic into what has been to this point a somber assessment of the difficulties of gaining even that modest measure of happiness which the universe is willing to permit, disrupts the novel for this brief but crucial period during the denouement.

Taken as a whole, however, *Far from the Madding Crowd* offers a mature view of life. The themes of Hardy's later novels are extensions of their early schematic expression in this novel. The other novels discussed in this study take tragedy for their major mode, as opposed to the subsidiary and undeveloped role that tragedy plays in *Far from the Madding Crowd*. In *The Return of the Native* and *The Mayor of Casterbridge* Hardy seeks a traditional pattern for tragedy which he can employ in a Wessex setting.

# 3

## THE RETURN OF THE NATIVE:

### *Opposites in Tragic Context*

*The Return of the Native* is Hardy's most imitative, most self-conscious, and generally least successful effort at high tragedy. In many ways an impressive novel—in concept of personality, in awareness of the symbolic value of setting—it is probably most accurately thought of as the kind of novel that a determined and self-taught writer had to get out of his system before he could go on to find his own manner. This is not to say that *The Return of the Native* is a "sport" in Hardy's *oeuvre*—far from it—or that Hardy did not repeat in later works many of the false notes in this novel, but that its distinctive qualities were blended in subsequent books with techniques and concepts of aesthetic form that were more of Hardy's own devising.

    *The Return of the Native* is the first of Hardy's sustained efforts at tragedy; its uncertainty may stem partly from Hardy's puzzlement as to how tragedy in fiction should be handled and partly from his lack of confidence that he could succeed. It is not surprising that Hardy looked to traditional concepts of the tragic in casting about for a method, even though his rustic scene and characters might have seemed of questionable promise when viewed in the perspective of the masterpieces of the past for which he had never lost his schoolboy's awe. That he imitated the pattern of classical tragedy is obvious in his use of the unities of time and place.[1] He also had originally planned the main action to take place in five books, to parallel the five acts of Elizabethan drama; and both Clym and Eustacia are fond of giving speeches that make their dilemmas external and theatrical. An allusiveness richer and more varied than customary in Hardy's novels elevates Egdon Heath into a setting appropriate for a drama of the widest significance. Indeed, Hardy's allusions draw upon the epic and heroic modes as well as the tragic, and encompass Norse and Indian as well as Greek, Roman, and Christian legend.[2] Hardy, then, encourages the reader to furnish literary recollection of tragic impact that amplifies the actions he presents. With the exception of *The Mayor of Casterbridge*, in which he borrowed another feature of traditional tragedy — the dominating hero whose very character expands the stage — Hardy never again relied so extensively upon his literary predecessors for examples of tragedy or for artificial extensions of plot and characters and situations.

Still, if Hardy had limited his efforts to classical patterns, it is not likely that *The Return of the Native* would have called forth the variety and quality of responses that it has. There is a basic difference between *The Return of the Native* and the more conservative imitation of classical forms, *The Mayor of Casterbridge*. Although interpretations of Henchard's story vary, the developments of dilemma and disaster are straightforward and unparadoxical. Attempts to define the emotional and fictive and aesthetic directions of *The Return of the Native* by any encompassing theory, on the other hand, constantly run up against complications and ambiguities within the text of the novel.[3] Hardy is attempting a fresh expression of tragic form, although one which incorporates the old patterns. His originality lies in his efforts to enlarge upon classical precept and to transpose the artificiality and rigidity of dramatic structure into the requisite freedom and tentativeness of fiction. Such elements as the unities of time and place are, naturally, only contributory to the novel's total effect. More important are Hardy's conception of tragic characterization and of the relationship between character and setting. In both Hardy is resourceful and suggestive, although his handling of them can be contradictory in the destructive sense of confusion or of being at cross-purposes as well as in the enriching sense of ambiguity.

# I

The uniqueness of *The Return of the Native* among Hardy's experiments in tragic form is that its two tragic protagonists — Clym and Eustacia — inhabit different psychic worlds and evoke from us different tragic reactions.[4] They resemble Antigone and Creon in that as tragic figures they draw upon different sources of vitality. They are distinguished from Sophocles' protagonists because they represent moral positions in a less rigid fashion. Rather than opposing social authority with the individual right to interpret moral necessity like Sophocles, Hardy constructs less absolute contrasts. Briefly, if abstractly, Eustacia's world is one of stature and ego, while Clym's is one of intention and society.[5] Each world possesses the conflicting qualities of stasis (stature and society, both established and accepted) and action (ego and intention, both striving to become recognized or fulfilled). The internal tension between stasis and energy in each character, as well as in the contrasts the characters represent, creates the sense of involvement and conflict which dominates their portrayal.

The distinctiveness of the values of Clym and Eustacia repeats, but in quite different terms, the contrast between the values of Sergeant Troy and those of the society personified by Gabriel Oak. Hardy uses the theme of cultural and psychic conflict in each of his great novels, but with differing devices. In *Far from the Madding Crowd*, Oak is so much more the man of attractive strength than Troy that aesthetic tension never rises to the pitch of tragedy where Oak is concerned. In a third context, Giles Winterborne in *The Woodlanders* is ethically superior to Fitzpiers, but is ineffectual against him, and again the effect is not similar to that in *The Return of the Native*. Clym and Eustacia represent Hardy's projection of the conflict of cultures into characters of equal attractiveness, who exert their appeals upon the reader by different means.

The stature of Eustacia is emphasized by Hardy in one of the famous chapters of purple writing in the novel. The "Queen of Night" chapter begins by asserting that "Eustacia Vye was the raw material of a divinity"; and Hardy goes on to develop this statement with a potpourri of allusions. He places Eustacia alongside goddesses (Artemis, Athena, Hera) and historical and mythological personages

(Alcinous, De Vere, William the Conqueror, Saul, Napoleon). He emphasizes her unconventionalism by calling her "pagan" and by pointing out that she had a youthful sympathy for Pontius Pilate's frankness and fairness. In all, Hardy describes her dignity, the grandeur of her black hair, her exaggerated expectations from life, and her refusal to compromise. She has, appropriately, a ruling passion, "to be loved to madness," which is raised to the level of a principle by being a longing "for the abstraction called passionate love more than for any particular lover" (p. 79).

The egoistic nature of Eustacia's existence, made evident by her disdain for a Wildeve rejected by Thomasin and by her wish to live an active social life in a resort town, is especially manifested by her attitude toward the heath. Although willing to grant that it has beauty, she is quite unable to accept its visual attractiveness as ameliorating its unpleasantness (p. 220). More tellingly, Eustacia sees the heath as directly opposed to her as an individual (p. 405). The heath, as the immediate object of Eustacia's paranoid hatred, becomes an image for Destiny, God, the colossal Prince of the World that she constantly blames for her unhappiness, which is clear from her final outcry, "O, how hard it is of Heaven to devise such tortures for me, who have done no harm to Heaven at all!" (p. 422). A mark of Wildeve's command over Eustacia's inner nature is when he reinforces this concept by reassuring her that "Fate has treated you cruelly" (p. 311; see also pp. 334, 404, 405) and that he, not she, is to blame for her predicament after Mrs. Yeobright's death and the consequent estrangement from Clym (pp. 372, 405).

The perspective of Clym's psychic world differs from Eustacia's from the outset. His characterization is based on idealistic intentions of speeding up social change, but he lacks the connotations of mystery and slumbering power of Eustacia that are developed through "Queen of Night." Disillusioned with the effeminacy and vanity of his Parisian vocation as a diamond merchant, Clym has decided to sublimate his worldly ambitions to higher aims. He intends to raise the intellectual quality of life among the heath dwellers without forcing them to pass through the intermediate stage of social ambition and worldly advance (pp. 203-04). This challenge to the established sequence of change and evolution makes him a figure comparable to Prometheus, who, thinking that mankind deserved some of the comforts of the gods, rebelled against the existing system even though it had placed him in high station. This similarity may be what Clym has in mind when he declares to Eustacia that he can "rebel, in high Promethean fashion, against the gods and fate as well as you" (p. 302), though by the time he says this he has become a furze cutter and seems not at all concerned that the opening of his school is being delayed.

The social reverberations which Clym's character causes depend upon his representativeness as well as upon his intentions. He represents two coexisting but separate societies, the heath and the outer intellectual world, which he had learned about in Paris and which had provided part of the rationale for his rejection of the life of business. The philosophies that those two societies impress upon Clym are not identical, but they are similar enough to separate further Clym's psychic state from Eustacia's. The two societies jostle for influence in Clym, but their impacts on his character are complementary. The basic point they have in common is the advocacy of self-abnegation, of submission to extra-personal forces: to principles, and to the overweening authority of the heath. The crucial differences in effect which the two systems have upon Clym are that as a neo-Parisian intellectual he optimistically intends to contribute to the spread of his principles, and that as a heath man he becomes a non-thinking passive exister. The effect of his early contact with the heath has been undermined by his adoption of the Parisian intellectualization of life, even though the concepts that follow his "rational" meditation upon existence are quite similar to those which he had absorbed from his years on Egdon. The healthy frankness of a philosophy of life based on direct experience with nature has been replaced by the murky generalizations and fears born of introspection in a closeted city life.

Clym's face, Hardy tells us, is typical of those modern men whose age is measured by experience and intensity of life (p. 161); his face reflects the effect of thought upon flesh as the mind is made to be aware of the "coil of things" (p. 162). The impetus for his return to Egdon has been his acquaintance "with ethical systems popular at the time" in Paris (p. 203). These systems are not identified, but if we can venture a guess about them from Clym's behavior, they are probably Fourieristic socialist schemes, St. Simonianism, and Comte's Positivism—all of which made the individual aware of his social role as his brother's keeper. On the other hand, Clym's intention to teach the heath folk how to skip a stage in their social evolution goes against a basic feature of these creeds—that the stages in the growth of a society are both observable and dependent on a necessary sequence—and therefore Hardy may have in mind other, less well-known philosophic creeds. (That there may be something superficial and faddish in being affected by "popular" systems of thought is largely beside the point in considering the qualities that make Clym's stance, or value-system, distinct from Eustacia's.) Because he is a man of the heath, he is as much its product as he is a product of Paris: his early society had been the human inhabitants of the heath, and "his estimate of life had been coloured by it" (p. 205). Indeed, his relationship with the heath itself had once been so close that Hardy makes a point of asserting that in the past one could not look at the heath without thinking of Clym (p. 198), a perspective that marks the intense interaction between man and environment. That the emphasis is upon thinking of Clym when seeing the heath rather than thinking of the heath when seeing Clym (a more natural and limited sort of associated thought) points up a symbiotic relationship that heightens the alliance between the man and his milieu, just as Oedipus' status in Thebes makes his guilt a condition for which the city is punished, that makes the city's "body" *his* body.

As the novel progresses, Clym loses some of his identity with the outer world: his face alters, losing its look of intellectuality as his "healthful and energetic sturdiness which was his by nature" begins to reacquire "its original proportions" (p. 243). By violating his civilized awareness of man's limitations—or, rather, by pursuing one society's concept of fit action in the environment of the other—he strains his eyes and can no longer read. When he goes to work cutting furze, he approximates his original status of co-identity with the heath (p. 298), so that not even his mother can readily recognize him as an individual (p. 328). The identification of Clym's specific "society," then, shifts; but there never is doubt that Clym, sensitive to the ideas around him, represents a societal orientation toward experience and knowledge; his intention is to bring together what he considers the most truthful and permanent features of his two societies.

The story of Clym and Eustacia has a powerful quality not only because they are at cross purposes with each other but also because neither one can achieve selfhood in the psychic world of the other.

But not all is negative. The dramas of their separate existences are possible because the physical world of the heath, of indeterminate character itself, can contain both, and provide the necessary testing of both. It is ironical that the discontent of Eustacia on the heath and the moral evolution of Clym during his acquaintance with Eustacia provide the emotional peaks and ethical significances of their lives. Hardy points out that if it were not for the isolating and purifying features of the heath, Eustacia would be vulgar and petty (pp. 78-79); if she and Wildeve had not died when they did, their lives would have been attenuated "to an uninteresting meagreness, through long years of wrinkles, neglect, and decay" (p. 453). We cannot know what Clym might have accomplished with Eustacia alive; but with her absent from his life he falls into pathetic ineffectuality, preaching religious cliches and commonplaces to an audience who come to hear him out of pity for his life rather than for the message he gives, for which there is not a word of approbation (p. 485). In the absence of conflicting and irreconcilable forces, life has become mediocre rather than noble and perpetually refreshed.

# II

The interrelationships of the heath and the major characters of *The Return of the Native* bear directly on tragic characterization. The indomitableness and stupendous impassivity of the heath constitute a benchmark helping to establish the moral position of the characters; the heath's permanence, representing elemental powers of the universe, is a stark reminder of the futility of human endeavor to alter one's lot. That it is the humble characters who are content to find small consolations in individual and social intercourse, and who abide on the heath in unquestioning resignation, enjoying the "triumph" in *The Return of the Native,* is Hardy's way of underlining the simplicity of the heath's relationship to the action of the novel.

On closer examination, however, it becomes clear that the heath is as much a cohesive force among characters as it is either a divisive agent or a sounding board that enables the gods or the reader to categorize the characters. Eustacia is as frequently identified with the heath through imagery, and with as much significance,

as Clym is through authorial statement. Amid an evocative description of the winds on Rainbarrow and Egdon Heath, which bear "a
great resemblance to the ruins of human song" (p. 60) and enable the
spirit of the heath to speak through the heath-bells "each at once"
(p. 61), Eustacia makes her first appearance and sighs. Although she
is thinking of Wildeve, and thus of the sort of seized happiness usually
considered antithetical to the heath's passive way, Hardy says that her
mood is identical to that of the heath:

> Suddenly, on the barrow, there mingled with all this wild rhetoric of
> night a sound which modulated so naturally into the rest that its begin-
> ning and ending were hardly to be distinguished. The bluffs, and the
> bushes, and the heather-bells had broken silence; at last, so did the
> woman; and her articulation was but as another phrase of the same dis-
> course as theirs. [P. 61]

Like the heath, she can be "passively still" while yielding herself to
the pull of a bramble (pp. 63-64). Her manner of dress in the winter-
time obscures her beauty like that of a tiger-beetle, "which, when observed in dull situations, seems to be of the quietest neutral colour,
but under a full illumination blazes with dazzling splendour" (p. 104).
She thinks the influence of Yeobright is like that of "summer sun"
(p. 146). These last-mentioned images are inconclusive, but Hardy
takes special pains, even using repetition, to indicate the relationship
between Eustacia and the heath in the scene that is the emotional climax of Eustacia's life. During her miserable uncertainty on her way to
elope with Wildeve, her inner state and the state of the heath are
peculiarly united by the storm. "Never was harmony more perfect
than that between the chaos of her mind and the chaos of the world
without" (p. 421); and "between the drippings of the rain from her
umbrella to her mantle, from her mantle to the heather, from the
heather to the earth, very similar sounds could be heard coming from
her lips; and the tearfulness of the outer scene was repeated upon
her face" (p. 421). Though it is given from Eustacia's point of view,
the sentence immediately following the latter quotation has misled
many readers of the novel: "The wings of her soul were broken by the
cruel obstructiveness of all about her." But that which is "about" her
is not only the material heath in itself. It is also her pride, her lack of
money, her being trapped between choosing an unworthy Wildeve

and a humiliating residence at her grandfather's house while waiting for Clym to reclaim her. (She is unaware that he has already written an apology.) The heath may in a large sense serve as a symbol of the circumstances of life which destroy the rebel; but it is simultaneously a manifestation of universal nature with which Eustacia is capable of being in full accord.

With a combination of instinct and culture that can manifest itself only in brooding or violence, Eustacia is an inverse parallel to Clym, whose countenance reflects both the heath and the modern ideas of Paris. The contrasting pattern between Clym and Eustacia has another ramification here. Eustacia, possessing qualities identical with those of the heath, expresses them in rebellion against her situation rather than in acceptance. Clym, possessing intellectual training, lets slip from him the social sophistication that made the mental training possible, in order to realign himself with natural forces. Although each is partly endowed with one of the qualities that would help to counteract the other's weakness, they can find no more common ground in their stances toward the universe than in their personal relationship, their stances toward each other.

Eustacia's rebellion is internal, even petty, for large sections of the novel, but rebel she does: in her affair with Wildeve (p. 79); obviously in her final decision to flee Egdon; more subtly in her refusal to tell the truth to Clym about the male visitor she had entertained on the day of Mrs. Yeobright's death. Her refusal to justify her actions may be passive, but it is hardly acceptance of her lot in the same sense in which Clym's exploitation of his blindness suggests the eagerness with which he postpones the sterner struggle of opening a school. Eustacia's adamant refusal to make the best of a bad situation is different only in degree from the attempt to destroy or escape from the situation. Her evident suicide is a further, and final, rejection of the circumstances that to her mind have conspired to keep her from the life she desires:[6] "[Wildeve is] not *great* enough for me to give myself to — he does not suffice for my desire! . . . If he had been a Saul or a Bonaparte — ah! But to break my marriage vow for him — it is too poor a luxury!" (p. 422).

The physical locations of Clym's and Eustacia's homes helped to form their characters even more markedly than is customary in Hardy's works. The lack of modulation or shading in Eustacia's perspective is predictable, for she has gone from fashionable Budmouth to the center of the heath (p. 143). That is, she develops her attitudes from the center of both of her worlds; she is given little freedom to observe modulations of life-styles. "There was no middle distance in her perspective: . . . Every bizarre effect that could result from the random intertwining of watering-place glitter with the grand solemnity of a heath, was to be found in her" (p. 78). Clym, on the other hand, was brought up on the periphery of two worlds, the heath and the meadow. The Yeobright home, Blooms-End, is on the edge of the heath, on the border of the cultivated land and the unclaimable land of Egdon (pp. 127-28). The meadow's softness, relative ease of life, and beauty give a different emphasis to the meaning of life and effort than that of lowering Egdon. Clym's borderland upbringing is reflected in the indecisiveness he manifests throughout the novel. In his youth he chose the bleak heath for an arena in which to act, a move which was not fated, for his father was a farmer; indeed, Hardy suggests that the choice was something of a perverse assault on the heath's impenetrableness. That in the heath's eyes the human Clym is a biological aberration is indicated by indirect parallelism. Clym's unnatural position in his adopted heath is matched by that of the "fir and beech plantation that had been enclosed from heath land *in the year of his birth*" (p. 246; my italics) and suffers "amputations, bruises, cripplings, and harsh lacerations" from a wind which on the open heath can merely wave "the furze and heather in a light caress" (p. 247). Like the plantation, Clym is "enclosed" from the heath's chastening and subduing power by his Paris experiences and by his advantageous living site at Blooms-End; like the trees, Clym is buffeted more by sufferings than are the native heath dwellers, who have neither expectations nor serious disappointments. Even Christian Cantle, who as his name suggests has been proselyted from the frank paganism of his peers, bears up tolerably well under the knowledge that women think him a "slack-twisted, slim-looking maphrotight fool" (p. 27).

The heath, then, has a much more complex function than is usually recognized. It is both a moral absolute and a universal solvent. Eustacia is not entirely an intrusion upon it, nor is Clym an utter familiar; indeed, to the heath indifferent to humanity, they possess equal value and meaning. The heath absorbs the Budmouth tastes of Eustacia and the Paris learning of Clym, and proves itself superior to both Budmouth and Paris as the inducer of a state of mind. It is a microcosm of the world or universe, but it is more inclusive than exclusive. The heath is not a detachable symbol, although Hardy's employment of the unity of place may create the effect that the heath is cut off from the real world by its isolated position and by the purity of its quality (its unique "heathness," as it were) as well as by an excessive harshness and indifference toward its inhabitants who possess consciousness. But it is not — or at least no more so than the settings for human effort in Hardy's other novels. The "testing" of Clym and Eustacia by their environment is little different from that of Tess by hers or of Jude or the Mayor by theirs. Indeed, Clym — the person most aware of the state of man's life — sees that the heath projects the same significance as crowded Paris. "There was something in its oppressive horizontality which too much reminded him of the arena of life; it gave him a sense of bare equality with, and no superiority to, a single living thing under the sun" (p. 245). "The arena of life" may not be a precise reference to Paris, but the tacit meaning of "reminded" underlines the point that the heath is an expansive setting, not an artificial limiting one.

# III

There is, obviously, more to Hardy's method of presenting characters of tragic import in fiction than has generally been conceded. The dramatist has certain advantages because he can expect the actor to provide some of the impetus to involvement, even though dialogue and conflict are what prove the ultimate worth of a tragic play. The novelist, on the other hand, finds he has a difficult choice to make when he purports to write a tragedy. If he emphasizes the expansiveness of the characters' actions by description and allusion, he runs the risk of being bombastic and sentimental; if he understates the complexity of his characters' behavior, assuming that the reader will be able to supply the requisite connotations, he runs the risk of being merely bathetic and of appearing lazy and indifferent to concrete expression. Hardy's overall tactic in *The Return of the Native* in the

face of this dilemma is to create appropriate concepts of key characters in chapters of set description and evocation, and thereafter to
allow the characters essential freedom with occasional allusion to
their grander status or with a brief restatement of their symbolic
values. This tactic is at least partly ironic, for the protagonists' actions
do not consistently justify the stature Hardy has attributed to them in
"Queen of Night" and "'My Mind to Me a Kingdom Is,'" and sometimes Hardy, apparently unintentionally, allows the characters' acts
to contradict their abstract values.

It is difficult to maintain balance in the pattern of alternating
sections of tragic connotations and character manifestation because
the two methods do not mix. When Hardy attempts to use both methods at once in an effort to heighten his characterizations by particu-
larizing Clym's or Eustacia's traits at a moment of intense feeling, he
risks producing flaws in the novel. Eustacia's dream after she sees
Clym for the first time provides an instructive example of Hardy attempting an ironic variation upon the pattern. He stresses the uniqueness of Eustacia's dream for a girl of her station, using a flurry of
mythological, classical, and contemporary allusions, with the evident
purpose of suggesting Eustacia's felt superiority to her unheroic surroundings:

> That night was an eventful one to Eustacia's brain, and one which
> she hardly ever forgot. She dreamt a dream; and few human beings,
> from Nebuchadnezzar to the Swaffham tinker, ever dreamt a more re-
> markable one. Such an elaborately developed, perplexing, exciting
> dream was certainly never dreamed by a girl in Eustacia's situation
> before. It had as many ramifications as the Cretan labryinth, as many
> fluctuations as the Northern Lights, as much colour as a parterre in
> June, and was as crowded with figures as a coronation. To Queen
> Scheherazade the dream might have seemed not far removed from
> commonplace; and to a girl just returned from all the courts of Europe
> it might have seemed not more than interesting. But amid the circum-
> stances of Eustacia's life it was as wonderful as a dream could be.[Pp.
> 137-38]

Despite this preparation, all we learn of Eustacia's exciting dream is
that it involved "transformation scenes." Hardy actually relates to us
only the dream that immediately follows the remarkable one. This

second dream is a "less extravagant episode" involving a knight in silver armor on the heath, clearly a projection of Eustacia's waking expectations of Clym. This second, conventional manifestation of fantasy, rather than supporting the grandioseness of Eustacia's character merely reinforces its mundaneness and substantiates the impression that she lacks a vital imagination. Still, it is quickly followed by the comment that "the fantastic nature of her passion, which lowered her as an intellect, raised her as a soul" (p. 139); and it is, after all, Eustacia's soul, not her intellect, that makes her tragic. But in referring to the dream, that which elevates her soul, Hardy does not give the unique dream but only the ordinary one. The larger question, then, seems to be whether Hardy can comprehend what kind of dream Queen Scheherazade might have or whether he thinks that to give the individualizing and aggrandizing dream in detail would have the unintended effect of limiting the tragic boundaries of Eustacia's character.

A clearer indication of how this description of Eustacia goes wrong can be found in a later, somewhat similar portrayal of Clym intended to reveal the superior qualities that make him a potential tragic hero. The portrayal of Clym, however, is more successful. When he first tells his mother that he is not going to return to Paris, he has no hope of having his motivations understood. He is "constitutionally beyond the reach of a logic that, even under favouring conditions, is almost too coarse a vehicle for the subtlety of the argument" (p. 207). A later discussion with his mother reveals to Clym that "he could reach her by a magnetism which was as superior to words as words are to yells" (p. 223). These passages about Clym, like those about Eustacia's dream, are based on the idea of a sensitivity so beyond the ordinary that its very possession sets one apart. Hardy, however, realizes that Clym's quality is beyond rhetoric, and he does not strain after expression to communicate Clym's specialness: he merely asserts, and relies upon the reader to supply the recognition. With Eustacia he promises, or seems to promise, the presentation of the mental process that demarcates her subconscious mind, but does not, in fact, present it. In the one case, then, he accepts the necessary limitations of his form for delineating the uniqueness of a tragic character; in the other, he seems to try to circumvent the limitations by implying that he is revealing more than he actually does. Whether Hardy's handling of Eustacia's dream is artistic charlatanry, magnificent failure, or diffusing irony is an issue that cannot be finally resolved. That Hardy is aware, at any rate, of the normal limitations of the form of fiction to express the verbally inexpressible is made clear in his comment on Clym's and Eustacia's emotional silence during a rendezvous: "No language could reach the level of their condition: words were as the rusty implements of a bygone barbarous epoch, and only to be occasionally tolerated" (p. 231). The mildly ironic tone of "to be occasionally tolerated" does not obscure the fact that Hardy is deliberately avoiding here the danger of using language to define a non-linguistic experience.

Although Hardy fails once with Eustacia, elsewhere powerful emotions appropriately go undefined. Dancing with Wildeve, Eustacia becomes rapt, evidently if not clearly with "rank" passion; "her soul had passed away from and forgotten her features, which were left empty and quiescent, as they always are when feeling goes beyond their register" (p. 310). Oddly, Hardy makes little of Eustacia's emotions in this scene other than to suggest indirectly that she possesses greater receptivity than the other female dancers because she experiences the "symptoms" of passion more powerfully than they do. In the ensuing conversation with Wildeve she is the circumspect — if proud and self-pitying — wife of a furze cutter. The principal value of the dancing scene is to substantiate the tragic potentiality of Eustacia.

When Hardy responds to the dilemma of tragic characterization by trying too hard to improve upon orthodox techniques of the realistic novelist, that is, when he experiments, we have seen that much can go awry. He also occasionally accepts too readily and too thoroughly the limitations to tragedy in fiction, that is, he fails to characterize as fully as necessary for basic acceptance in terms of verisimilitude. Such under-characterization is nearly a signature of Hardy's art. More than any other important novelist of his time, he encourages the reader to supply motivations and explanations for his characters' acts. This habit can be functional at times. The evil of Alec d'Urberville becomes part of the threatening universe; Sue Bridehead becomes the final bane of Jude because he cannot, any more than can the reader, comprehend the vagaries of her tortured consciousness. Even the "Inconsequence" that Felice Charmond personifies does not fully account for her self-sacrifical and impassioned behavior in *The Woodlanders*, and she thus is elevated beyond the

stereotype of a *femme fatale* to a character capable of being destroyed in the same manner that Giles is, the unintended victim of the
love of her life. But under-characterization can also harm a fiction.

An example of unsatisfactory truncated characterization in *The
Return of the Native* is found in the skein of Clym's early actions. The
early stages of his growing love for Eustacia are too scantily traced
for the reader to understand the point Hardy is making about the
novel's title character. From the time of his suspicion that the Saracen
Knight is a woman (p. 170) to his telling his mother that he has given
up his plan of offering "with my own mouth rudimentary education to
the lowest class" (p. 227), there is but one hint of the nature of Eustacia's attraction to Clym — the trite, unexceptional attraction of
beauty (p. 220). The flaw I am suggesting is not in the nature of the
attraction itself, for Hardy emphasizes the unusual beauty of his
heroine, but in that Hardy has not given us a clear enough look at his
hero for us to know the nature of the effect that an emotion like
sensual attraction can have upon him. Hardy has told us that Clym in
his returned state represents modern thinking man. Does he then
mean to imply that modern man's efforts to think are inevitably futile
because he is still prey both to animalistic drives and to man's tendency to idealize his drives? Or is he implying that Clym's posture as
a conquering hero over ignorance and oppression is essentially but a
pose, and that Clym's pretensions to selfless nobility are as hollow as
Eustacia's claims to temporal social superiority? Hardy's "characterization" of Clym over the course of his courtship of Eustacia can be
taken to "mean" any of these things, and other things as well, simply
because Hardy has given no indication *what* Clym's immediate capitulation to beauty represents, either universally or individually. Nor is
it clear whether this barrenness of motivation is intended to elevate
Clym to a tragic level through simplicity or whether the barrenness is
intended ironically to disrupt Hardy's pretensions that his novel is a
tragedy by suggesting an incoherence in Clym's psyche.

# IV

Many readers feel that Hardy is playing a massive joke on them in suggesting that an ill-starred love affair between a petulant girl of nineteen and an indecisive philosopher and social reformer can convey a meaningful comment on man's situation in the universe.[8] And it is true that apart from the introductory chapter on Egdon Heath, "Queen of Night," and "'My Mind to Me a Kingdom Is,'" the narrator explores only briefly the two characters' exceptional natures. Richard Carpenter remarks, with "Queen of Night" in mind, that "Hardy appears for long stretches to forget that his heroine is anything more dignified and grand than a passionate woman caught in a web spun by circumstances and her own emotions."[9] Carpenter's following remark — "as the story unfolds, the tone shifts from tragic elevation to ironic pathos" — is a concise statement of a skeptical reader's opinion of the success of Hardy's method of characterization in this novel.[10] Carpenter in effect overlooks the possibility of Hardy's use of the fairly standard technique of fiction to establish a characterization early in the narrative and permit the character to act freely in the later parts without authorial manipulation. Hardy clearly has intended to demonstrate initially the quality of Eustacia's rebellious nature through classical allusions, and then through more dramatic and objective methods to show her making choices that substantiate the authorial presentation. Some choices are deliberate and conscious (such as her lighting the bonfire on the first anniversary of her affair with Wildeve), some mainly unconscious (such as her rejecting Wildeve when she learns that Thomasin may prefer another lover to him); but all of them are consistent with the overriding static portrayal of her as an imperious woman of passion and impulse, and consistent with her active state as a woman struggling to achieve the sort of recognition her ego demands of life. Moreover, as I have observed, tragic expression in *The Return of the Native* arises only in part from classical allusions and the actions and motivations of the principal actors; more complex feelings are created through the conflict of irreconcilable modes of psychic existence.

Nevertheless, Carpenter and other readers are certainly correct in pointing to a level of mundaneness in Eustacia. Her attitudes are intensely social in the sense that she desires parties, fashionable clothes, and friends of similar tastes, not in the sense that Clym's ideas are societally significant, dealing as they do with justice and the organization of a citizenry toward cultural goals. Eustacia's rebellion against the higher powers rests upon a subjective claim to special consideration because of her beauty: "She had cogent reasons for asking the Supreme Power by what right a being of such exquisite finish had been placed in circumstances calculated to make of her charms a curse rather than a blessing" (p. 305). The context suggests irony: "To an onlooker her beauty would have made her feelings *almost* seem reasonable" (my italics). In her last, great speech she says that destiny has prevented her from being a "splendid" woman (p. 422); this may have connotations of grandeur, but she means only that as the runaway paramour of Wildeve, who is no Napoleon or Saul beyond the reach of social law, she cannot hope to glitter in a Continental social scene. In all, then, Eustacia's tragic authority is limited exactly because her own perspective is so myopic. The dignity implicit in enunciating an attack upon Heaven in her last speech does not survive unscathed a cool appraisal of the puniness of her goal. Perhaps none of these or other undercuttings by Hardy prove conclusively that Eustacia is less than tragic, but they keep her from being tragic in the grand manner, as Hardy's explicit characterization of her gives us good reason to expect her to be.

Nor is Clym free from ironic diminishment, primarily because his allegiances are so varied—to a Paris-founded modern system of idealism, to the heath's absorptive power, to his mother, to his final guilt-ridden missionary vocation. Easily diverted from his selfless plan to educate the heath people, vacillating among various plans of action —none of which he ever decisively chooses—Clym's intention to correct the world's ills is flexible to the point of self-parody. His failure to understand that his pursuit of private happiness with Eustacia goes against his self-conceived societal role forestalls his intentions before he can even decide upon the most basic implementation for them. He thus presents a character less unified than Eustacia's, whose only disputed allegiance is between that part of her which is a complement of the heath and that part which vehemently loathes the heath for its lack of superficial society.

The uncertainty of the source of tragic authority in the novel is partly the result of the ambiguities in Hardy's structural scheme of two psychic worlds. Clym's instability of interests weakens both his individuality and his representativeness, further dissipating the possibilities for tragic resonance in his sufferings. The problem of locating a center for the awareness of truth frequently present in tragedy is also complicated by these factors — that is, by the structural scheme and by the evidences of inadequate purpose in the protagonists. But, of equal significance, awareness of truth is hindered because Eustacia and Clym come to individual awarenesses of man's role in his own fate which are exactly inverse to the conclusions that are appropriate for them. Clym is weak and easily frustrated; nevertheless, difficulty in his relations with his mother and Eustacia has been mainly their fault rather than his. To blame himself for their deaths, which he does, means he misses part of the truth of his experience. He thinks that he "must have been horribly perverted by some fiend" not to have gone to make up the argument with his mother (p. 367), but he blames himself, not the "fiend." It is clearly for the wrong reason (in Hardy's presentation) that Clym denies that malignity in the supernatural has brought about his ultimate sorrows:

> He did sometimes think he had been ill-used by fortune, so far as to say that to be born is a palpable dilemma, and that instead of men aiming to advance in life with glory they should calculate how to retreat out of it without shame. But that he and his had been sarcastically and pitilessly handled in having such irons thrust into their souls he did not maintain long. It is usually so, *except with the sternest of men*. Human beings, in their generous endeavour to construct a hypothesis that shall not degrade a First Cause, have always hesitated to conceive a dominant power of lower moral quality than their own; and, even while they sit down and weep by the waters of Babylon, invent excuses for the oppression which prompts their tears. [P. 455; my italics]

Eustacia, at the opposite extreme, pities herself as unfairly manipulated by adverse forces, though she has made all the decisions that in her final scene eventually place her on the heath with no choice but death or dishonor. The manner of portraying her lamentations and diatribes against Fate suggests that she has inadequate insight into her own blameworthiness. Hardy says that she hates the "disagreeable" as much as the "dreadful" (p. 353), and strongly hints that the blame she levies at the "indistinct, colossal Prince of the World" would be directed more accurately toward herself:

> She had certainly believed that Clym was awake [when his mother had come to call], and the excuse would be an honest one as far as it went;

but nothing could save her from censure in refusing to answer at the first knock. Yet, instead of blaming herself for the issue she laid the fault upon the shoulders of some indistinct, colossal Prince of the World, who had framed her situation and ruled her lot. [P. 353][11]

This fairly late reference to Eustacia's self-delusion reinforces the impression given in an early description of her that she suffers from paranoia. "She could show a most reproachful look at times, but it was directed less against human beings than against certain *creatures of her mind*, the chief of these being Destiny" (p. 79; my italics). Thus, one of the bases of Eustacia's tragic stature — her consciousness of being a sufferer — can reasonably be interpreted as meretricious.[12]

Clym's potentiality as a tragic hero is revived briefly toward the end of the fifth book, but then is adversely affected by the sixth, which was added at the request of Hardy's magazine editor. At the end of book 5, on the morning after the deaths of Eustacia and Wildeve, Clym comes to a recognition of a basic feature of the tragic universe — the realization that there are offenses beyond law's power or prerogative to punish:

"I am getting used to the horror of my existence. They say that a time comes when men laugh at misery through long acquaintance with it. Surely that time will soon come to me!"

"Your aim has always been good," said Venn. "Why should you say such desperate things?"

"No, they are not desperate. They are only hopeless; and my great regret is that for what I have done no man or law can punish me!" [P. 449]

The implied question — what to do with one who is immune from man's law — has answers applicable to *The Return of the Native*. One is that justice rather than law might be applied in this instance. (Perhaps this justice would implement such human supra-legal agents as Hardy refers to earlier in the novel. Commenting on Venn's firing shotguns to keep Wildeve away from Eustacia and thus keep him faithful to Thomasin, Hardy writes, "The doubtful legitimacy of such rough coercion did not disturb the mind of Venn. It troubles few such minds in such cases, and sometimes this is not to be regretted. From the impeachment of Strafford to Farmer Lynch's short way with the scamps of Virginia there have been many triumphs of justice which are mockeries of law"[p. 321].) Another answer to the implied question is that the guilty person can punish himself. Neither answer is by itself perfectly satisfactory, because each implies an epistemological limitation upon experience, a limitation based on the idea that there is an ultimately right fate assignable according to identifiable grounds. This sort of rationally assignable fate works against the sense of ineffable unease at the "due" fate suffered by the protagonist in tragedy, an unease prompted by the inextricableness of individual responsibility and the responsibility of forces beyond the individual, the effects of which within his own life he is nonetheless accountable for.

Had Hardy not tried to take Clym beyond his expression of despair and guilt at the end of book 5, there would be some justification in putting Clym forward as the principal tragic hero of the novel. At this point there is a powerful measure of mystery to Clym's condition and his likely fate. Clym is caught up in the awareness of his blame in Eustacia's death, while the reader has just been made deeply conscious through observation of Wildeve's and Eustacia's last thoughts that Clym is not alone to blame. Had the last stage in the reader's consciousness of the story been this, there would be at least the possibility of an unease similar to that produced by the conclusions of *Oedipus Rex* and of Shakespeare's plays. But to carry the story past this point raises the expectation that some further aspect of the inextricableness of responsibilities will be developed through action. Such a development does not occur, the purpose of book 6 being to satisfy an editor's sense of simplistic poetic justice (moreover, a poetic justice that does not include the novel's major sufferers) rather than to round out Hardy's tragic vision of life![13] (The marriage and happy life of Thomasin and Venn in book 6 also disrupt what seems to have been Hardy's original scheme — to have their relationship parallel the Clym-Eustacia relationship of irreconcilable worlds. As Hardy writes in the 1912 footnote to the third chapter of book 6, Venn "was to have retained his isolated and weird character to the last, and to have disappeared mysteriously from the heath, nobody knowing whither — Thomasin remaining a widow." That a parallel had been intended by Hardy is impossible to confirm; but it fits into Hardy's mechanistic early concepts of plotting and of contrasting sets of characters.)

To carry on the narrative after the principal action has ended is in itself enough to curtail much of the tragic effect. The adequacy of Clym for the role of tragic hero further depends upon the nature and scope of what he has learned; that is, whether his knowledge evokes an expanse of meaning beyond the applicability of the knowledge to his own individual condition. Such an expanse of meaning is not even remotely presented in book 6. Clym's realization and his subsequent actions, though full of psychological relevance in emphasizing his death wish and cementing his dedication to his mother, have only a deflating effect upon his tragic potential. In accepting guilt and in large part putting aside the justice/law dilemma, Clym makes a far from adequate response to the question of his undeserved immunity from legal punishment. Clym's half-insane guilt is already implicit in the last pages of book 5, but if Hardy had left the matter open by not dwelling in book 6 upon this sense of guilt, Clym might have retained some of the rich complexity essential for tragic characterization. Of course, that Clym mistakenly emphasizes *his* guilt instead of the guilt of the universe does not improve his tragic standing merely because the ambiguity of justice and law remains unresolved. That justice is not further explored by Clym in book 6 is important because it shows that he has been beaten down by his suffering rather than made aware by it.

# 4

## THE MAYOR OF CASTERBRIDGE:

### *The Moment as Repetition*

If *The Return of the Native* can be thought of as a student's idea of tragedy, with Hardy borrowing features from and alluding to classical stories, *The Mayor of Casterbridge* is perhaps best approached as the work of a man at once a schoolmaster and an innovator. Hardy did not know what to do with all of the tragic tradition he inherited and tried to marshal in *The Return of the Native*, and the structure is overladen with reminders of analogies. With *The Mayor of Casterbridge*, Hardy knew what to accept from tradition, and how to incorporate his borrowings into a vital structure. In *The Return of the Native*, the setting has an uncertainness, as do the relationships between characters and between characters and their environment, which is not overcome by Hardy's self-conscious elaboration of a potentially tragic situation. *The Return of the Native*, for all its brilliance in conception and frequent brilliance in execution, presents a blurred aesthetic experience. But in *The Mayor of Casterbridge*, Hardy avoids committing again the artistic errors of *The Return of the Native*. The setting is less metaphysical but no less suggestive; and as opposed to the double focus of Clym and Eustacia, Henchard far exceeds Farfrae as a concentrator of aesthetic effect. Hardy also organizes the interaction of plot and character and allusions so skillfully that this novel both successfully follows classical precedent and stands indepen-

dently as an example of universal tragedy. The basic plot situation of
*The Mayor of Casterbridge*, with its emphasis upon the single protagonist and upon the course of the hero's downfall, is patently Aristotelian; the plot also derives, perhaps making it more influential in its
appeal, from the vision that places man against man, and individual
man against the universe, with nothing for him to rely upon, finally,
but whatever he has inside himself.

  Two quite different structural features dominate the presentation of *The Mayor of Casterbridge*; yet the result is not aesthetic
chaos but a remarkable unity. That these two structural features do
not work against each other attests to the primacy of the thrust of
both toward the demonstration of the universality of the tragic action.
One works on the large scale of a theory of history: the presentation
of an individual struggle as but one occurrence of timeless rhythm,
the cycle of change within the organization of society; the other compresses the entire action into a single portion of the novel's plot. The
compressed scene points up the tragic import in the novel's materials,
even though an extension of the understanding of a single part into a
perception of the meaning of the overall movement of the novel must
remain tentative. Tragedy and the idea of social change develop together in *The Mayor of Casterbridge*, although the idea of a cycle and
the idea of the tragedy of Henchard are not synonymous: the course
of Henchard's tragedy continues after he has completed his term within the cycle.

# I

*The Mayor of Casterbridge* gives a detailed survey of the process of
change, which is embodied in the portrayal of the transfer of the po-
tency and influence that distinguish the figure of authority from the
mass of mankind, in a manner that prefigures changes in the social
organization. The characters who possess these qualities, Henchard
and Farfrae, project Hardy's reading of the historical process.

  That the process of change is one of Hardy's major concerns
here is indicated by the preciseness with which the novel sets forth
alterations of strength. Whereas the other Wessex novels offer only

three phases of change — existence of an authority or a social mode; a challenge to it; and its reaction, usually a retreat — *The Mayor of Casterbridge* contains a succession of subtle gradations of activity: creation of an authority; the consolidation of its power; its weakening; and its collapse. Moreover, we observe these gradations in nearly two full sequences. Both Henchard and Farfrae follow this pattern individually. Collectively, the actions and fates of the two men connote the recurring nature of human action, and further imply that the seemingly unavoidable enmity between Henchard and Farfrae has antecedents, and will recur continually in other men with conflicting manners of life. The repetitive action in *The Mayor of Casterbridge* communicates Hardy's view that human history is not linear but cyclic, and that the dominant motif of movement is not steady and unwavering progress but pulsating and irregular advances. He states this opinion explicitly in non-fictional writings.

In the apology prefixed to *Late Lyrics and Earlier* (1922), Hardy refers to Comte's concept of progress occurring not in a "straight line" but in a "looped orbit."[1] Three decades earlier while discussing movements in art he had written in greater detail about the concept: "Things move in cycles; dormant principles renew themselves, and exhausted principles are thrust by." This "periodicity . . . does not take the form of a true cycle of repetition, but what Comte, in speaking of general progress, happily characterises as 'a looped orbit': not a movement of revolution but — to use the current word — evolution."[2] Obviously Hardy draws a distinction between the ideas of a cycle as a "looped orbit," by which he predicates change, development, and progress, and as a "true cycle of repetition," by which he evidently means mere nonaccretive redundancy. He rejects the purely static quality of classical cyclicism, instead looking to the evolutionary meliorism of man's lot.

The total action of *The Mayor of Casterbridge* suggests that there is improvement when Farfrae replaces Henchard as the mayor and leading citizen of the agricultural town, but that improvement in ultimate matters is not extensive. The novel's setting — amid the remains of several cultures whose qualities have helped to shape modern life — sustains the enunciation of a concept of history. The characters of Farfrae and Henchard are formulated by Hardy in terms that clearly make them parallel figures, so that — whatever else one may say they are—it is not a distortion of aesthetics to observe that they express elements of an abstract idea. But at the same time, Hardy eschews the blatant approach of the allegorist. Structural presentation of character, especially Farfrae's, softens the pedantic impact of the novel's theme. Hardy postpones a clearcut presentation of Farfrae, an essentially secondary character in that he is no match for Henchard in attracting reader interest, and thereby prevents a simplistic reduction of him to a cardboard figure in a schema.

The perception that the heroes' lives exemplify an abstract theory arises in good part upon their confronting a common situation, the necessity to establish a relationship with their environment. The character and manner of behavior of Henchard and Farfrae are given substance by the context in which they appear; Casterbridge measures the worth of these striving individuals and the comparative value of the qualities each possesses by presenting similar situations and opportunities to each. Both Henchard and Farfrae come unbidden into the low-keyed, season-based life of the Casterbridgeans, Henchard after abandoning his search for Susan, Farfrae on his way to the New World. Neither has a significant past he is willing to reveal to his associates. Henchard remains silent because of shame and awareness of the enormity of his offense against Susan in selling her while he was drunk; Farfrae effectively if less intentionally, and quite purposelessly, disguises his true individuality behind patriotic sentimentality. Both are regarded as curiosities by the passive residents of the country town, Henchard for his hardness in business dealings, Farfrae because of his fervorous singing at the Three Mariners tavern. That neither becomes assimilated into the groups of men among whom he works and whom he leads is early made clear—Farfrae in the Three Mariners cannot comprehend the easy, humorous lamentations of the workmen (pp. 59-63), and Henchard in his tactless impetuosity humiliates his workman Abel Whittle for an inability to rise early enough in the morning to meet his schedule (pp. 112-14). These early scenes are only initial indications of the heroes' separateness from the town. Neither man has any friends among the Casterbridgeans; and though Abel Whittle prefers Farfrae to Henchard for an employer, there is little evidence that the townspeople's reaction to Farfrae's fall would differ much from their blandly distant acquiescence in Henchard's ("They wondered and regretted his fall" [p. 254]). Indeed, with Farfrae's rise, the towns-people's sense of affection and their easy familiarity toward him drop away, and are replaced by a willingness to mock his wife by revealing her past with a skimmington (p. 309).

Coupled with the homologous relationship of Henchard and Farfrae to the society of Casterbridge is their possession of a crucial quality of effective authority. As the muted competition between them breaks into direct confrontation with Farfrae's purchase of a small corn and hay business, Hardy describes both men in the context of his famous paraphrase, "Character is Fate, said Novalis" (p. 131). What they have in common is "energy": Henchard's "amazing energy" accounted for his financial success, and had been the basis for the Corporation electing him mayor (p. 129); Farfrae's "northern energy" had overmastered "the easy-going Wessex worthies" (p. 131).[3] Energy is Henchard's primary strength, and it has been sufficient to permit him to obtain wealth and prestige in the Casterbridge he had entered twenty years before. Energy alone would be sufficient to enable him to retain his position, if he had still to contend only with Caster-bridgeans. He does not begin to fail until Farfrae arrives. While his failure may be triggered by the simultaneous arrival of his guilty past in the person of Susan, it more obviously develops from his incapacity to better Farfrae within the scope of activity that he is accustomed to dominate.[4]

In addition to the energy which he and Henchard seem to have in equal degree, Farfrae has other qualities which enable him to triumph over Henchard. Farfrae possesses insight that allows him to evaluate the alternatives during his thrustings for success; Henchard has doggedness, which blinds him to any method but direct personal action (p. 132). Farfrae is deliberate and patient, Henchard impulsive and impatient. The interaction of these qualities ruins Henchard and makes Farfrae wealthy in the grain-buying season of uncertain weather. The same season reveals Henchard to be erratically super-stitious, first in following and then in abusing the weather prophet's accurate prediction, and Farfrae to be rationally self-reliant and cautious in dealing in many small lots of grain and thus making a num-ber of modest but consistent profits.

The pattern of change in The Mayor of Casterbridge relies upon the related qualities in Farfrae and Henchard. Their personal-

ities show how certain admirable and effective traits lose their efficacy when confronted by the superiority of other, contrasting traits.
Hardy, emotionally committed to the values of the Casterbridgeans
but thoroughly aware that the world in which those values were respectable was rapidly shrinking even at the supposed time of the tale
(the 1840s), accepted change and even acceded to the principle of
progress. Thus, as Henchard falls to Farfrae's strengths, the world
makes a slight advance because of a single individual's ability to uti-
lize modern techniques in an ever-increasingly complex environment.
It is generally understood that the Casterbridge financial world judges
the relative effectiveness of Farfrae and Henchard. What has not
been adequately understood is that Farfrae has weaknesses that in
turn leave him open to challenge and destruction by a being slightly
superior to him.[5]

Farfrae falls far short of perfection, although he represents an
advance beyond Henchard in certain qualities that determine their
worldly success and failure. Farfrae and Henchard have moral shortcomings of the same type but of different degrees and manifestations.
Their deficiency in matters of human feeling isolates both men within
themselves. Henchard is the sterner man, but he is not as removed
from sympathy as Farfrae at the end of the book.[6] Throughout his
decline Henchard becomes progressively more aware of and more
tolerant of others' wishes, mainly because he fears to alienate Elizabeth-Jane. Farfrae, on the other hand, although he possesses the insight that allows him to be a step ahead of the fluctuations in the corn
and hay market, does not exercise this insight in his close personal
relationships. He ignores Lucetta's request that they leave Casterbridge, and, more generally, he again and again misconceives
Henchard's feelings and motives concerning him. And so the forces
of the cycle continue to operate. According to the logic of the cyclic
theory, Farfrae is doomed to fall in time, and the fall will be brought
about by the permanent characteristics of his nature rather than by
artificial factors relating to a particular time and place. As Henchard's
flaws were always capable of precipitating disaster, his situation
lacking only the appropriate opposition, so are Farfrae's.

But, again, Hardy does not allow the shifts in position of the
two men to become an allegorical minuet. It is not instantly recognized that Farfrae is as blemished as the man he supplants. The novel's

structure tempers the presentation of the cyclic nature of change. By delaying significant authorial comment on Farfrae until late in the tale, by masking Farfrae's less congenial qualities, Hardy promotes fairly complex reactions to Farfrae's personality and behavior. Against the early, dark background of crude indifference to suffering and the high-handed tactics of Mayor Henchard, Farfrae strikes one favorably, certainly as a fitting person to found a new way of doing business. His little kindnesses toward the defeated Henchard are documented with special care. Thus, when the narrator's voice is finally employed to convey criticism of Farfrae, the natural impression is that Farfrae's personality is changing in the course of the novel, under the pressures of his new circumstances (although, as we shall see shortly, his characterization is clarified rather than altered).

The effect of a change of this type taking place over the length of the novel does not, of course, run counter to cyclic theory, for psychological change itself may be viewed as inevitable in the sense of the political-moral cliché, "Power corrupts." Indeed, the manner in which *The Mayor of Casterbridge* illustrates the cyclic theory is the more impressive because Hardy draws both upon the idea that moral failure follows upon worldly success and upon the awareness that the grounds for a man's destruction are innate in his individual selfhood. The intellectualized cyclic view easily absorbs both aspects, for to the Positivist theorist Comte the important consideration is not the how or the why of the recurrence of historical event, but the fact of it.

Still, the choice that Hardy makes—to increase the sense of change in Farfrae during the course of the novel rather than to present him throughout as clearly flawed, a man little better than Henchard except in his business skills—forestalls a facile understanding of an abstract theory. The potentially stiff organization of a major thematic motif is circumvented; and the novel acquires a quality of ambiguity that would have been lacking had Hardy made clear from the start that Farfrae is not as sterling a character as he first appears to be.

Hardy manages narrator intrusiveness so that no direct analysis of Farfrae's character is offered until after Henchard's total ruin, and after the last person associated with his pre-Farfrae life (that is, Lucetta) has left the scene. This analysis necessarily comes late in the

novel, since Henchard has maintained his forcefulness for some time
after his bankruptcy. He is progressively stripped of personal reso-
luteness only after he loses his wealth and position. He realizes that
he is not revengeful enough to unmask Lucetta directly by telling
Farfrae that he had been Lucetta's lover (p. 284); his rendezvous with
Lucetta in the Roman Amphitheater makes him realize that he no
longer envies Farfrae's possession of such a weak and foolish woman,
even though he still is envious of her great love for him (pp. 289-90);
and he realizes in the granary loft that he cannot bear to harm Farfrae
physically (p. 315). Henchard thereupon becomes, finally, a passive
hanger-on. After he acknowledges, in drawing back from killing Farfrae, that his overthrow by Farfrae is complete, Henchard's ambition
shifts. From a wish to regain his lost prestige and wealth, his main
hope now becomes the retaining of Elizabeth-Jane's love. At this
point, when the tension has been removed from the competition between Henchard and Farfrae, and when Farfrae assumes a more
directive role appropriate to his socio-political eminence, the narrator directs the reader to the fissures in Farfrae's glossy character.

   The clearest indication of Hardy's attitude toward Farfrae appears here, just after the reversal of the positions of the two men has
become absolute. After Lucetta's death with its aftertones of disgrace,
Farfrae goes into a "dead blank," but only briefly. He is not one of
those men who has a "dogged fidelity" to an image or cause after his
judgment has reversed an earlier decision. Significantly, Hardy adds
that without such faithful men "the band of the worthy is incomplete."
Farfrae's nature—with its "insight, briskness, and rapidity"—makes
him soon realize that "by the death of Lucetta he had exchanged a
looming misery for a simple sorrow" (p. 348). Shortly, Hardy's diction
extends the impression of aridity in Farfrae's emotional life by suggesting how thoroughly his character is permeated by the values of business: meeting Elizabeth-Jane on a walk, he turns an "appraising" gaze
on her (p. 352). Though she evidently satisfies his criteria, the diction
pinpoints Farfrae's business-like attitudes even in personal affairs. In
portraying this encounter, Hardy subtly criticizes the Scot by a reference to his "undulatory accents" and by the ironic stage direction
indicating that Farfrae alludes to the dead Lucetta's secret "with the
pathos of one of his native ballads" (p. 352). This keen allusive irony
is honed further by the subsequent suggestion that Farfrae's sentimen-

tal attachment to his homeland is at least partly affectation. At his wedding to Elizabeth-Jane, Farfrae sings of "his dear native country that he loved so well as never to have revisited it" (p. 373) — a much more sarcastic way to indicate Farfrae's mixed practical and romantic feelings about Scotland than the previous references to those feelings (pp. 62-63, 183). Two other indications of Farfrae's emotional limitations occur during the search for the vanished Henchard after the wedding: Elizabeth-Jane and Farfrae decide not to travel too far because Farfrae remarks that to stay overnight away from home "will make a hole in a sovereign" (p. 381);[7] and his comment after hearing Abel Whittle's extended description of Henchard's final sufferings and death is that of a man utterly incapable of perceiving any grandeur in human experience: "Dear me — is that so!" (p. 384).

The natural idea — fostered if not created by Hardy's delay in making the narrator's views of Farfrae known — is that Farfrae is a man corrupted by success, whose natural feelings have been frozen by financial dealings. But while there may be a measure of truth in this idea, its suggestion of deterioration in Farfrae's character insufficiently acknowledges the subtlety with which Hardy has put forth the qualities of this second "mayor of Casterbridge." Hardy's attentions to Farfrae's character toward the end of the novel make clear a characterization that he had hinted at throughout. Farfrae's character, like Henchard's, is consistent. His shortcomings are inborn; it is only the deeper concern with Henchard's character that prevents a prompter definition of Farfrae's. Hardy offers many clues to Farfrae's character, but they do not fall into place until the later chapters are read. An inspection of the earlier part of the novel will allow us to make out more clearly the stuff that Farfrae is made of.

The affection offered by Henchard upon their first acquaintance is returned by Farfrae only in a general, if frank, fashion. Henchard pleads great and mysterious affection as his reason for encouraging Farfrae to stay in Casterbridge (p. 73); Farfrae, on the other hand, agrees mainly because he recognizes the opportunity. That this is his motivation is made clear by the much later parallel scene in which Farfrae is offered the mayoralty just as Lucetta has nearly persuaded him to leave Casterbridge. Illogically pleading helplessness by saying, "It's ourselves that are ruled by the Powers above us!" (p. 280), Farfrae demonstrates that vanity overrules his affection

for Lucetta; in a similar way his earlier rationalization for capitulating
to Henchard's urgings—"It's Providence! Should any one go against
it?" (p. 73)—undermines the sense of the "liking" he feels for Henchard (p. 88). Farfrae's obvious desire to be mayor in face of Lucetta's
anxiousness to leave Casterbridge is an unmistakable amplification of
the nascent vanity suggested by his reaction to Henchard's first appeal to him to remain in Casterbridge: "The young man appeared
much moved by Henchard's warm convictions of his value" (p. 56).

Capable of more sophisticated techniques than he is usually
given credit for,[8] Hardy in one early passage employs a near-Jamesian
sensitiveness.to scene in order to provide an oblique insight into Farfrae that acquires full clarity only after the reader reflects upon
Farfrae's behavior toward the end of the novel. Henchard opens his
heart to his new manager in discussing his indecision concerning the
Jersey woman now that his long-lost wife has returned, and Hardy
presents Farfrae objectively throughout the long scene. Farfrae says,
"I'll be glad to hear it, if I can be of any service." But in an ostensibly
extraneous bit of scene-painting—the only such "digression" in the
chapter—Hardy portrays Farfrae's state of mind by describing how he
allows "his eyes to travel over the intricate wood-carvings of the chim-
ney-piece, representing garlanded lyres, shields, and quivers, on either
side of a draped ox-skull, and flanked by heads of Apollo and Diana
in low relief" (p. 88). His distraction by the irrelevant details of the
chimneypiece implies at the beginning of their association that Farfrae is indifferent or reluctant to become as intimate as Henchard's
confessional attitude would seem to invite. The description, of course,
has certain obvious reverberations in the succeeding pages of the
novel. Henchard loves music, he and Farfrae use financial weapons of
war, Henchard saves Lucetta and Elizabeth-Jane from a bull, and
the phrase "Apollo and Diana" ironically looks forward to the ultimate marriage of Farfrae and Lucetta, the Jersey woman of
Henchard's story (or, perhaps more appropriately for "Diana," it hints
at Farfrae's and Elizabeth-Jane's marriage). But in the context in
which it appears, that is, the relationship between Henchard and Farfrae, the description shows how willing Farfrae is to be diverted from
a direct and undivided consideration of others' human troubles.

Even Farfrae's early acceptance of his loss of Lucetta, which
Hardy uses to make clear the limitations and shallowness of his per-

sonality, is foreshadowed. On his first, highly charged meeting with Lucetta, he puts aside the brimming sentiments he feels in her presence when he remembers a business engagement (pp. 186-87); and on his wedding day he delays his return to Casterbridge and his reunion with his bride of a few hours because he "had been detained by important customers, whom, even in the exceptional circumstances, he was not the man to neglect" (p. 245).

Some of Farfrae's narrowness in personal relations can be condoned. He is not, after all, the villain of the piece. The frequent coolness of his emotions is not so much hypocritical as it is an accompaniment to the precise objectivity displayed in his career; he has, as Lucetta says to him, "both temperatures [warm and cold, passionate and frigid] going on in [him] at the same time" (p. 183). That a young man would answer Elizabeth-Jane's "wise little remarks" with "curtly indifferent monosyllables" in preference to the "more Protean variety" of Lucetta's "phases, moods, opinions, and also principles" (p. 200) can surprise no one very much; and indeed his impulsive infatuation with Lucetta is itself a highly skillful element of characterization. With it, Hardy allays the uncongeniality inherent in Farfrae's machinelike common sense. Still, that Farfrae would pay a courting visit to Elizabeth-Jane preparatory to proposing, and then be immediately infatuated by Lucetta's sophistication, displays not only his ability to shift directions in the middle of a situation but also his lack of intensity in emotional attachments. Having rationally settled on the "thrifty" and "pleasing" Elizabeth-Jane (p. 181), Farfrae falls prey to the excess of sentiment that elsewhere he manages to fit into the occasion, for example, in his songs of home. Farfrae, unlike Henchard, is not destroyed, partly because of the ironic fortuity of his wife's death. But his weakness—his inability to manage his feelings consistently—makes clear that the only major "cyclic" factor in the novel is Farfrae's command of modern machinery and business techniques.

Henchard falls before Farfrae's superior business talents. He recognizes during the fight in the loft that his superior physical strength has become irrelevant. Henchard, being the man he is, cannot conquer in a business world that contains a Farfrae. What Hardy leaves unsaid, but what is obvious from his characterization of Farfrae, is that Farfrae himself can be toppled by a man who combines business acumen and sympathetic insight into humanity, or who simply is more clever professionally than he is.[9] The second cycle, or "looped orbit," possesses all of the elements necessary for completion except the appearance of the conquerer of Farfrae. The novel's unity is dependent both on the final destruction of Henchard and on Farfrae's arriving at a position in his cycle at the end of the novel which is analogous to Henchard's at the beginning of the relationship between the two men.

I have not discussed the centrality of Henchard in *The Mayor of Casterbridge* in order to emphasize Hardy's handling of the cyclic structure. Certainly Henchard is a more dynamic and unifying figure than Farfrae. In failure he expands the reader's awareness of human complexity and misery more profoundly than can Farfrae in triumph; even were he to be portrayed in defeat, Farfrae has not the extremism and amplitude of character from which tragedy draws its power. But in terms of functional structure, Farfrae is not much inferior to Henchard. Both are manifestations of the forces that within the novel reveal the inevitability of perpetual conflict and change. Their personalities and interaction define the cyclic design of the novel, and release the tragic forces which their energies fail to protect them against.

# II

The second structural feature of *The Mayor of Casterbridge* reinstates Henchard to his correct central position. It is he who makes the decisions — and who comes to the tragic awareness — in the plot event that epitomizes the values and meanings implicit in the entire action of the novel. The encapsulation of an entire literary work into a brief sequence is not rare, of course. The better the writing the more implicitly does *every* scene imply the relationship it holds with the totality of structure in which it appears. Obvious examples of single scenes whose contents express the meaning of the work as a whole are Gregor's waking to learn he is a bug in *The Metamorphosis*, Ahab's nailing the gold piece to the mast of the *Pequod* in *Moby Dick,* and Strether observing the meeting of Chad Newsome and Mme. de

Vionnet in *The Ambassadors*. *The Mayor of Casterbridge*, then, is not unusual in its employment of the condensed sequence that reveals the values and standards by which the characters measure themselves and by which they are measured by the implied author. Hardy's use of the condensed sequence is important here because of its resolution of ambiguities in the larger tragic action of the novel. The principal condensed sequence almost literally repeats, and certainly epitomizes, the major plot action of the novel, that is, the concentration of events surrounding the visit of the Royal Personage to Casterbridge. That visit, with Henchard's eccentric behavior and Farfrae's manhandling of Henchard in order to assert the correct order of welcome, is the most crucial scene in the sequence and the focus of the entire action of the novel. Henchard in this scene — for of course the interest is still with him rather than with either Farfrae or the Royal Personage — conducts himself for the last time in the role of Mayor of Casterbridge. It is an utterly self-deluding role, for Farfrae has become the second immigrant Mayor of Casterbridge and in thus completing the upward movement of his cycle has completely ursurped Henchard (p. 281). But the scene with the Royal Personage is for Henchard's career both encapsulation and climax.

Placing this scene in its context makes evident how it compresses the novel's tragic action. Shortly before the scene with the Royal Personage, the following events have occurred. Henchard has gone to work for Farfrae as a day laborer in the barns and granaries; he has begun to drink again, having fulfilled his vow of twenty years of abstention; he is told that Farfrae is responsible for the failure of the town council to set him up in the seed shop; and, after the meeting with Lucetta in the Roman Amphitheater during which he ceases to envy Farfrae his prize, he returns Lucetta's letters by means of Jopp. Jopp opens the poorly sealed package and reads the letters to the drinkers in Peter's Finger tavern before he takes them to Lucetta. Those who hear the letters begin to plan a skimmington for which the expenses are partly paid by Newsom, who is passing through Casterbridge at night on his way to Falmouth in search of Susan and Elizabeth-Jane.

By the time the chapter describing the visit of the Royal Personage opens, then, a number of plot skeins have ended, and the beginnings of other skeins have been prepared. By surrendering Lucetta's letters, Henchard willingly deprives himself of his last weapon against Farfrae's peace of mind; and with characteristic heedlessness of other people's possible malignity he has put that weapon into the hands of a man whose moral decline he has materially contributed to, and who has — though unknown to Henchard — a recent grudge against Lucetta (p. 291) as well as a long-standing resentment toward Henchard himself. Hardy's intention to link the skimmington with the visit of the Royal Personage is indicated by the opening sentence of chapter 37: "Such was the state of things when the current affairs of Casterbridge were interrupted by an event of such magnitude that its influence reached to the lowest social stratum there, stirring the depths of its society simultaneously with the preparations for the skimmington" (p. 302).

The central place of this chapter in the exposition of Henchard's decline and the promise of Farfrae's is evident in the way the visit is promulgated. Henchard of course is living on the threads of respectability; he has only his own pride to provide him with the self-respect he had previously held as the natural concomitant of the respect accorded him because of his position as mayor. The Royal Personage is heralded both as a neo-Farfraean and as a seal of approval for the evolutions in agricultural practice introduced by Farfrae: "He had consented to halt half-an-hour or so in the town, and to receive an address from the corporation of Casterbridge, which, *as a representative centre of husbandry*, wished thus to express its sense of the great services he had rendered to agricultural science and economics, by his zealous promotion of designs for *placing the art of farming on a more scientific footing*" (p. 302; my italics). Hardy reminds the reader of the cyclic-tragic status of Henchard in describing Henchard's clothing when he appears before the Council to request to be allowed to receive the visitor: "Henchard entered the room, in clothes of frayed and threadbare shabbiness, the very clothes which he had used to wear in the *primal days* when he had sat among them" (p. 303; my italics). The royal visit is clearly part of the cyclic pattern, contributing to Henchard's tragic course, rather than one of the plot incidents that Hardy complained were made necessary by his weekly serialization (though the appearance of a man of royal blood — even one who does not say a word — may have raised the social tone of the novel in the eyes of conventional Victorian novel readers).[10] Other

indications of Hardy's effort to make the royal visit connotative are
the disruption of the ritualistic time for the drinking of their daily
pint by Solomon Longways and Christopher Coney from eleven
o'clock to half-past ten (p. 304), and Elizabeth-Jane's quick perception that the sight of Henchard approaching the royal carriage with
a private Union Jack was less a sight for terror than it was a "spectacle" interesting for its being "a strange phenomenon" (pp. 306-07).
(Elizabeth-Jane's reaction might be seen as a forecast of her eventual
coolness to Henchard once she learns that he had deceived Newsom
[pp. 364-65], but it is more reasonable to interpret it structurally, as
a means of alerting the reader to a significance in Henchard's behavior.)

　　If one were to pick a single instant that compresses the novel's
entire action, it would be the paragraph that immediately follows the
description of Elizabeth-Jane's reaction:

> Farfrae, with Mayoral authority, immediately rose to the occasion. He
> seized Henchard by the shoulder, dragged him back, and told him
> roughly to be off. Henchard's eyes met his, and Farfrae observed the
> fierce light in them despite his excitement and irritation. For a moment
> Henchard stood his ground rigidly; then by an unaccountable impulse
> gave way and retired. Farfrae glanced to the ladies' gallery, and saw
> that his Calphurnia's cheek was pale. [P. 307]

This is the last authorial reference to Henchard in this chapter. Not
until the next chapter does Hardy mention that after Farfrae's rebuff
Henchard withdrew behind the ladies' stand of chairs to stare abstract-
edly at the lapel of his coat where Farfrae had seized him. The rest
of chapter 37 takes up the lead of the last sentence in the above quotation to deal with Lucetta's prideful denial to her female neighbors
that Henchard had ever helped her husband find a place in Casterbridge, and to be concerned with the lower classes' guarded
references to the skimmington that they are planning for that evening.
The chapter concludes, then, with reminders that the hero's position
at the top of his cycle is never secure. Part of his insecurity stems
from the masses' growing indifference to the hero's happiness once
he has gained supremacy. Most of the poorer inhabitants of Casterbridge no longer view Farfrae as possessing "that wondrous charm

which he had had for them as a light-hearted penniless young man, who sang ditties as readily as the birds in the trees." They have less "anxiety to keep him from [the] annoyance" of seeing his wife's effigy in a skimmington than they would have had "in former days" (p. 309); and it falls to his employees to send Farfrae on a false business trip to get him out of town during the time for which the skimmington is planned (see pp. 318-19). Another cause for the hero's insecure position is the direct animosity of the less successful toward the triumphant; Jopp borrows from Aristotle to explain why the evening of the royal visit is the most appropriate time for the skimmington mockery: "As a wind-up to the Royal visit the hit will be all the more pat by reason of their great elevation today" (p. 309).[11] The first paragraph of the next chapter suggests how great that elevation has been in the public consciousness with the reference to the "chit-chat" overheard by Lucetta "that her husband might possibly receive the honour of knighthood." That the chit-chat is ill-founded does not alter the relevance of the "intoxicating *Weltlust* [that] had fairly mastered" Lucetta (p. 310).

After chapter 37 the role of the royal visit in working out the tragedy of Henchard and the cycle of change which he and Farfrae embody is clarified (pp. 310-33). Those post-climatic events bring Henchard to a recognition of the actuality of his status and provide justification for hinting at Farfrae's own ultimate overthrow. The weakness in Farfrae that will lead to his overthrow can be quickly mentioned here, because he is not the center of attention; rather it is Henchard who is nearing the climax of his tragic cycle. Farfrae's strengths are his caution and his knowledge of scientific farming methods; his weakness is his lack of understanding of human relations. The skimmington exploits this weakness, revealing publicly that the caution he had employed so successfully in business dealings had been cast away in choosing a mate. Inexperienced with women, he has turned aside from Elizabeth-Jane, who would have been a natural complement to his own personality, to choose a woman who teases him and flirts with him on their first meeting. Lucetta's arch remark near the end of their first conversation, "Dear me, I feel I have quite demoralized you!" (p. 187), characterizes her importance in Farfrae's cycle. The point is not that Farfrae should have conducted an investigation into Lucetta's past, as he might have done before buying a new business. After all, a need to investigate Elizabeth-Jane's past is never suggested: her illegitimacy means nothing to Farfrae even when he hears of it, though Hardy uses her illegitimacy to cast an aspersion (undeserved, in this novel) on social mores (p. 368). The point has to do with the implications of Farfrae's ineptness in dealing with people whose personalities are in any marked degree different from his. Moreover, his willingness to accept Lucetta's death indicates the shallowness of his human attachments. There is also no grief on his part for the unborn child that dies with Lucetta; in Victorian context, this lack of interest in a "living reminder" of the loved one is a further mark of Farfrae's emotional limitations. The plans for the skimmington proceed apace with the royal visit and are spurred on by that visit and by Farfrae and Lucetta's prominence in welcoming the Personage. Farfrae's ultimate but unobserved downfall, then, is inextricably bound up with the completion of Henchard's fall.

The determination of the extent of Henchard's downfall, and Henchard's realization that it has occurred, concern most of the rest of the day of the royal visit. It is significant that Henchard has been thrust down by Farfrae in the presence of genuine royalty—as if to suggest the factitiousness of Henchard's claim to heroic stature, perhaps, but more importantly to suggest by association the kind of social stature that Henchard feels he deserves to come in contact with. In the loft, Henchard finally acknowledges the overthrow of his own "reign." But not surprisingly, that acknowledgement must be prepared for. Henchard has not immediately recognized what has occurred through Farfrae's collaring him in the presence of royalty. He first rationalizes his retreat from Farfrae and the royal visitor—"I took it like a lamb, for I saw it could not be settled there" (p. 311)—but he also realizes in a paranoid but not inaccurate fashion that the evil fortune that has seemingly settled on him as a result of Farfrae's appearance in Casterbridge has come to a head: "After being injured by him as a rival, and snubbed by him as a journeyman, the *crowning degradation* had been reserved for this day—that he should be shaken at the collar by him as a vagabond in the face of the whole town" (p. 311; my italics). The phrase *crowning degradation* suggests that Henchard realizes that the tragic circumstances of his life have been capped; nonetheless, he sets out to do battle with Farfrae. It is he who selects the field for the battle; significantly, he chooses his own grounds (the granaries had been his before they were Farfrae's), whose advantageousness for himself he had already surveyed (see p. 274). He defeats Farfrae in a battle of physical strength in which he uses only one arm; but he delays the murder in order to tell Farfrae why he is to die — "this is the end of what you began this morning" (p. 315) — and looks into Farfrae's eyes again, as he had that morning; this time he recognizes the truth of his situation, total defeat, and says:

> "Your life is in my hands."
> "Then take it, take it!" said Farfrae. "Ye've wished to long enough!"
> Henchard looked down upon him in silence, and their eyes met. "O Farfrae! — that's not true!" he said bitterly. "God is my witness that no man ever loved another as I did thee at one time. . . . And now — though I came here to kill 'ee, I cannot hurt thee! Go and give me in charge — do what you will — I care nothing for what comes of me!" [P. 315]

Henchard's defeat is portrayed through his declaration of love for Farfrae, through his recollection of "that time [of their first acquaintance] when the curious mixture of romance and thrift in the young man's composition so commanded his heart that Farfrae could play upon him as on an instrument," and through Hardy's description of Henchard's crouching posture on the sacks of grain after Farfrae has left — "Its womanliness sat tragically on the figure of so stern a piece of virility" (p. 316). These passages, together with descriptions of Henchard's throwing his arm roughly across Farfrae's shoulder during their early friendship, have encouraged some readers to see homosexuality as a cause for Henchard's downfall. There is some usefulness in this suggestion, for it helps explain something of Henchard's mysterious self-isolation and his strained personal relationships: he never seems to have a physical desire for Susan, even after eighteen years of regret for his cruel treatment of her, and his desire for Lucetta partakes much of pride of possessing a rare and courted object and only briefly of customary romantic or sexual love (pp. 169-71, 201, 205). (A further striking circumstance overlooked by Victorian Mrs. Grundys is Henchard's living alone with Elizabeth-Jane in affectionate relationship after he knows that she is not his daughter.

Their ages are proximate enough for sexual feelings—twenty and forty. That readers have never, to my knowledge at least, noted the potential scandal of their living under the same roof is testimony to Henchard's amorphous sexual quality.) Throughout the novel Henchard has more affection for Farfrae than for any woman. When Farfrae muses to Lucetta that Henchard's animosity toward him is more like "old-fashioned rivalry in love than just a bit of rivalry in trade" (p. 279), a reader versed in abnormal psychology might well feel that the rivalry is with Lucetta for Farfrae's love rather than with Farfrae for Lucetta's affection. But to stress the potentially sensational aspect of Henchard's character in this manner is to misunderstand seriously the reasons for the success of the novel as tragedy. To turn Henchard into a latent homosexual whose downfall stems from an inability to maintain the latency may stimulate fresh readings of the novel; but it does not help us to understand either the formal or the emotional qualities of the novel.

These descriptions of Henchard and his use of the language of love at the moment of his recognition of final, utter defeat are important because they echo Henchard's own scornful opinion of women as weak (see pp. 288-89), and because they have an ironic reflection upon his early friendly contempt for the physical slightness of the Scotsman Farfrae (pp. 87, 103-04). In this scene of defeat, Henchard talks in the language of love to a man, which at least places him in a potentially feminine role, and is described by Hardy as "womanly." In relation to the pattern of tragedy, the "feminine" Henchard is by his own definition a weakened man. Since his effective attributes have been bare energy and perseverance, the final triumph by Farfrae's intellect is signaled by Henchard's refusal to persist in the exertion of his energy.

Once Henchard recognizes that he has been totally supplanted by Farfrae, he is able to accept other alternatives to the kind of life he had experienced when he was successful. He feels Farfrae's distrust of him at the lonely crossroads when Henchard had stopped Farfrae's gig to tell him that Lucetta is dangerously ill. Farfrae's suspicion causes Henchard to lose self-respect, "the last mental prop under poverty," whereupon he "cursed himself like a less scrupulous Job" (p. 330). He is able, now, to recognize the transient goals he had pursued in competing with Farfrae. "So much for man's rivalry, he thought,"

when he hears Elizabeth-Jane say that the shock from seeing the skimmington will likely kill Lucetta (p. 331). Thereupon—still on the
evening of the royal visit and the fight with Farfrae—Henchard trans-
fers his affection from Farfrae to Elizabeth-Jane: "Above all things
what he desired now was affection from anything that was good and
pure. She was not his own; yet, *for the first time*, he had a faint dream
that he might get to like her as his own,—if she would only continue
to love him. . . . He called [at Farfrae's] as much on Farfrae's account
as on Lucetta's, *and on Elizabeth-Jane's even more than on either's*.
Shorn one by one of all other interests, his life seemed centring on
the personality of the stepdaughter whose presence but recently he
could not endure" (pp. 331, 333; my italics).

# III

The effect of this sequence — which has taken almost as long in the
explication as in Hardy's telling — is to compress the major tragic action of the novel into a brief span. Hardy's ability to do this is central
to the power of all his novels, but in none is it so well adapted to the
framework of the story as in *The Mayor of Casterbridge,* and in none
does the intensity created by the compression contribute so markedly to the success of the tragedy of the protagonist. The events of
the royal visit indicate the conditions of Henchard's and Farfrae's
competition as well as the tragic and cyclic connotations of that competition and its conclusion. Henchard's ultimate doom is presaged in
his acquiescence to his situation; his role in expressing cyclic change
is over. Yet, the story of Henchard's life is not complete. Here, on this
matter of the point of completion, the cycle of change and the tragedy
of Henchard diverge. The cycle goes on continually; Farfrae's position
within his cycle affects his presentation in the later parts of the novel.
But the on-going movement of the cycle has left Henchard behind.

The last part of the novel concludes the tragedy of his life with
a method similar in type but different in degree from that which I
have been discussing, that is, the ramifications of a single scene in
relation to the entire action. Now I would suggest that the last part of

Henchard's life—and the last part of his tragedy—is in basic points a repetition of the first part. Specifically, his betrayal of Newsom in telling him falsely that Elizabeth-Jane has died is a nearly exact reenactment of his betrayal of Susan in selling her.

Numerous parallels reinforce Henchard's second violation of moral order as a repetition, and a reflection, of his first. Even the language of the two scenes coincides to stress their relationship. Henchard acts on "impulse," "in pure mockery of consequences," expecting to be unmasked in five minutes and to be cursed by Newsom, who then would take Henchard's "last treasure" from him (p. 338). Similarly, after he had sold Susan, he was "surprised and nettled that his wife had taken him so literally" (p. 17). And as with his repentant search for Susan after he had sold her, Henchard now rushes out of his house after he realizes that Newsom had believed him, only to see Newsom depart in the same coach he had alighted from half an hour before. As Henchard watches Newsom depart, the narrator reflects that Newsom's "simple faith in Henchard's words [was a] faith so simple as to be almost sublime...[a] trust so absolute as to shame him as he stood" (pp. 338-39). The simplicity in Newsom repeats a similar forthrightness in Susan, whose "freedom from levity of character, and the extreme simplicity of her intellect" permitted her to believe "that there was some sort of binding force in the transaction" in the furmity tent (p. 17). A more precise echo of the phrase describing Newsom's trusting nature occurs in Henchard's thoughts about Elizabeth-Jane's mother just before he goes into his self-imposed exile: "His wronged wife had foiled [his attempts to replace ambition by love] by a fraud so grandly simple as to be almost a virtue" (p. 367). It is also relevant that Newsom, again like Susan, is not inclined to blame Henchard severely for his acts. The returned Susan advances her claims quite meekly, willing to go away from Casterbridge when she misinterprets Henchard's comment that he wishes not to acknowledge her as his wife (p. 84. Henchard wants to remarry her instead); Newsom takes Henchard's part as soon as Elizabeth-Jane begins to criticize her stepfather for his deception: "'Twas as much my fault as his, poor fellow!" (p. 365).

Another similarity between the lie to Newsom and the selling of Susan strikes me as being particularly noteworthy, especially in view of the battering that life has dealt Henchard to this point. In much the same manner that he had attempted to hide the sale of his wife, Henchard tries to "keep the position he had accidentally won" (p. 339). Thus, just as the sale of Susan had been his first act in defiance of a life limited by other people's legitimate demands on him, so is his lie to Newsom the "last defiant word of a despair which took no thought of consequences" (p. 347). The upshot of the parallelism between these two events is that Henchard as a personality had not been entirely put down, even though his role in the cyclic pattern of change ended as he allowed himself to be thrust aside in the presence of the Royal Personage. It is the consequences of the lie to Newsom that finally require the death of Henchard, although he is dying not just for the lie to Newsom but equally for the sale of Susan, which is indicated by a final series of parallel notations in the two events. As Henchard flees Casterbridge upon the well-founded suspicion that Elizabeth-Jane is about to meet Newsom and cast off Henchard from her affections, he acknowledges his blame: "I — Cain — go alone as I deserve — an outcast and a vagabond. But my punishment is *not* greater than I can bear!" (p. 361). This passage is an elaborated, but unmistakable, reenactment of Henchard's earlier response to the sale of Susan: "He must somehow find her and his little Elizabeth-Jane, and put up with the shame as best he could. It was of his own making, and he ought to bear it" (p. 17).

Perhaps the way the later violation of moral order echoes the earlier helps to keep the reader's sympathy for Henchard in spite of his lie to Newsom and his continued deception of Elizabeth-Jane about her parentage. Henchard is seen through this echoing as a man who reacts to circumstance according to his character — a strong man ready to absorb greater opposition than he receives, and then laying himself open, willing to accept full blame for what unexpectedly results. The self-involved Henchard expects others to defend themselves as vigorously as he does himself; and when they do not, he is at a loss as to how to put himself once more into accord with the mass of his fellowmen. Nevertheless, it is significant that Henchard's tragic self-awareness is made complete only after he flees Casterbridge. In his worldly condition he has come full circle, and Hardy — offering another variation on the idea of cyclic change — suggests that Henchard now could begin the reascension and topple Farfrae, that he has gained what he had lacked before, and what, evidently, Farfrae does not have:

And thus Henchard found himself again on the precise standing which he had occupied a quarter of a century before. Externally there was nothing to hinder his making another start on the upward slope, and by his new lights achieving higher things than his soul in its half-formed state had been able to accomplish. But the ingenious machinery contrived by the Gods for reducing human possibilities of amelioration to a minimum — which arranges that wisdom to do shall come *pari passu* with the departure of zest for doing — stood in the way of all that. He had no wish to make an arena a second time of a world that had become a mere painted scene to him. [P. 369]

Even after this wisdom is attained by the protagonist, Hardy has still to arrange for Henchard's death, to complete his tragic course, and to obtain for the atmosphere of the story the aesthetic discipline and emotional bitterness that his will affords. Hardy is also concerned with the last pronouncement of the novel, Elizabeth-Jane's musings about the necessity to limit expectations. It may have little value for the reader who believes that Elizabeth-Jane's rather mild sufferings do not merit her the dignity of having the final word;[12] still, it is an appropriate coda to the narrative of Henchard, and implicitly to the future course of Farfrae: "Happiness was but the occasional episode in a general drama of pain" (p. 386). In Elizabeth-Jane's comment, the cyclic pattern of slow modification of society is coupled with the tragic course of an individual's life. Although the tragic character is forced by his character and situation to strive, and although society benefits from his exertions, Henchard experiences only ultimate rejection and destruction; society discards him for another leader. In this novel, to a greater degree than in Hardy's other works, every expression — not just Elizabeth-Jane's concluding remarks — circles back to the fundamental meaning of the story. In *The Mayor of Casterbridge* the unity of the story develops from Hardy's selection of formal techniques that in themselves express the thematic issues.

# 5

## THE WOODLANDERS:

### *Tragedy in Common*

When Thomas Hardy settled into his new house, Max Gate, to write *The Woodlanders,* he had been an active novelist for a decade and a half, his fame still due mainly to *Far from the Madding Crowd.* After its success, Hardy had varied his subjects because he wanted to avoid being "typed" as a novelist of rural scenes. In fact, he had put off writing a "woodlands" story immediately after *Far from the Madding Crowd* for that reason; how much of the plot of that early story he employed in the first novel he wrote in Max Gate is unknown. He had tried military and philosophical novels, social comedy, and short stories; but these evidently gave him little pleasure, for he seldom mentioned them in his later years. He had hit upon his true métier, tragedy, in *The Return of the Native,* but, disappointed in its critical reception, went back to writing "mere" serials on a variety of subjects and moods.

In *The Mayor of Casterbridge,* the novel written just before *The Woodlanders,* Hardy attempted tragedy again. The critical reception again was not enthusiastic, but Hardy may have felt more confident as an artist because of the skill with which he had handled the tragic form of *The Mayor of Casterbridge.* It may well be that he was becoming weary of trying to write novels that would please the public's taste and decided instead to write stories that would enable him to develop his obsessive themes. In any event, he thereupon embarked on a sequence of experimental tragic fictions whose continuing subject is the animus of society against the individual. *The Woodlanders* expresses some of the most important elements of Hardy's analysis of the role of social pressures on man's chances for happiness: the explicitly microcosmic nature of the setting, Wessex; and the overall sympathy given to all sufferers, no matter what their merit according to conventional moral evaluation. These elements are incorporated in the novel primarily in the structuring of the character relationships. Though a successful experiment in the development of tragic expression, *The Woodlanders* is the least acclaimed of Hardy's great novels — partly, I think, because critics have not paid heed to the experimental nature of any of Hardy's novels, preferring to think of him as a traditional tale-teller,[1] and more particularly because *The Woodlanders* fits so awkwardly into most concepts of fictional genre.[2]

There is little doubt that in *The Woodlanders* Hardy intended to compose a tragedy. He early enunciates conditions in the Hintocks that he finds appropriate to tragedy. The essential condition of the fictional world is, for Hardy, that it be capable of sustaining a universal action. The Hintocks are described as being

> one of those sequestered spots outside the gates of the world where may usually be found more meditation than action, and more listlessness than meditation: where reasoning proceeds on narrow premises, and results in inferences wildly imaginative; yet where, from time to time, dramas of a grandeur and unity truly Sophoclean[3] are enacted in the real, by virtue of the concentrated passions and closely-knit interdependence of the lives therein. [Pp. 4-5]

*The Woodlanders,* then, is intended to illustrate the potential for tragedy in humble surroundings, that is, in the lives of any group. Not only are man's surroundings in the novel universal in space; they are also universal in time. The temporality is extended by the reference on the opening page to "charioteers" (that is, Romans) who had once lived in the "sequestration" of the Hintocks. Continuity among generations is established by descriptions of "the ante-mundane Ginnung-Gap believed in by [Marty's] Teuton forefathers" (p. 15), the early Georgian architecture of Melbury's house (p. 25) and the time-worn initials of "bygone generations of householders" which are carved into its doorjambs (p. 51), the old packs of cards whose great stains had been produced "by the touch of generations of damp and excited thumbs, now fleshless in the grave" (p. 88), and the eagerly participated and half-believed in Midsummer Eve conjuration of glimpses of future husbands (pp. 171-75). This union of present particularity and timeless universality is a common Hardy quality, utilized especially in *The Mayor of Casterbridge* in depictions of the Roman Amphitheater, and in the portrayal of Mai-Dun Castle in "A Tryst at an Ancient Earthwork" (*A Changed Man*).

That events in the Hintocks are significant beyond simple manifestation helps to emphasize the microcosmic character of Hardy's materials. Hardy connects the lowly actions of Giles and Marty to a global scale in stating that "their lonely courses formed no detached design at all, but were part of the pattern in the great web of human doings then weaving in both hemispheres from the White Sea to Cape Horn" (p. 21). This sort of rather portentous philosophy belongs to the sophistication of *The Dynasts* far more than to the plain-spokenness of *The Woodlanders* but, Harvey Curtis Webster to the contrary,[4] "the great web of human doings" is not deterministic. What Hardy intends by the phrase is the panorama of human activity, of which he arbitrarily has selected a small portion to examine. The interdependence of lives in the "great web of human doings" expands organically by use of nature imagery, with the inclusion of animal and plant life as parts of the interdependent, because universally suffering, universe. Not only are natural scenes portrayed through human imagery ("The bleared white visage of a sunless winter day emerged like a dead-born child") but animals are activated by human qualities, as when they "discreetly" withdraw until nightfall from the scene of human activity (p. 24). The principal concern in the novel, human love, acquires ironic shadows, and the agitations of its participants are mocked when love is equated with animalistic sex that ends in ashes and sickness of heart (pp. 168, 232). In the earlier Wessex novels, nature's repose is a rebuke to man's agonized consciousness; in *The Woodlanders,* the agony is shared, caused in both spheres by mutual destructiveness. On the human level, transitory happiness acquired by some characters plunges others into despondency; on the non-human level, animals prey on smaller animals, and trees gouge each other for survival.

Hardy gives a grim picture of nature preying on nature — owls catch mice, rabbits eat wintergreens, and stoats suck the blood of rabbits. He emphasizes the suffering in nature (trees "disfigure" one another by rubbing against one another in their "wrestling for existence" |p. 376| ), as well as portraying nature's apparent enmity toward man (the bough strikes Giles's hut during a storm as if it were "the mouth of an adversary," and the rain that follows is as "blood from the wound" [p. 372] ). All this creates an atmosphere of universal malice and destructive egoistic energies which can only be seen as intentionally antithetical to Victorian romanticism. Darwinism is more pervasive in *The Woodlanders* than in Hardy's earlier novels. Only in one way do the tragic situations of humanity and nature differ: natural entities answer to no religious law and know of no social sin (see pp. 350, 369).

The specific "variety" of tragedy that Hardy treats in *The Woodlanders* portrays the source of life's misery as a quasi-transcendental condition of life, the expression of which suggests determinism, but whose operation is more accurately thought of not as pre-fated but simply as the consequence of the interaction of natural forces struggling for life and supremacy.[5] As Giles walks through the woodlands in pursuit of Melbury and Grace on their way to a sale of trees and faggots, the omniscient author reflects on the common "fating" agent:

> They went noiselessly over mats of starry moss, rustled through interspersed tracts of leaves, skirted trunks with spreading roots whose mossed rinds made them like hands wearing green gloves; elbowed old elms and ashes with great forks, in which stood pools of water that overflowed on rainy days and ran down their stems in green cascades. On older trees still than these huge lobes of fungi grew like lungs. *Here, as everywhere, the Unfulfilled Intention, which makes life what it is, was as obvious as it could be among the depraved crowds of a city slum.* The leaf was deformed, the curve was crippled, the taper was interrupted; the lichen ate the vigour of the stalk, and the ivy slowly strangled to death the promising sapling. [Pp. 58-59; my italics]

The universality of the force is emphasized by Hardy's reference to a "city slum" in conjunction with the leafy woodlands. All mankind, all nature — as we have seen, both sensate and without feeling, both willing and without evident volition — are subject to this Unfulfilled Intention. "The identity of the Little Hintock woods

appears less to be a face like Egdon Heath than a force, less a countenance to be misread than the corrosive energy which in its
'Unfulfilled' course can be comprehended as a prophetic pattern for
all human striving."[6]

The arena for tragedy erected by Hardy for *The Woodlanders*
has, of course, traditional boundaries. It has antecedents in *Oedipus
Rex,* in which the hero's intentions of aggrandizing his reputation for
wisdom dissolve into horrible futility upon gaining true knowledge,
and in *Antigone,* where Creon intends to be obeyed at whatever cost
to human feeling. Frustrated intention informs Hardy's favorite kind
of story; its variegated manifestations create the disparities of hope
and achievement in *The Mayor of Casterbridge* and *The Return of
the Native* as well as in the later *Tess of the d'Urbervilles* and *Jude
the Obscure.* One can even see a certain justification for the theory
in Hardy's life; the man who had intended to be a poet found himself
writing serials for family magazines. A sort of bafflement of benevolence shapes much of the action and imagery in *The Woodlanders.*
There are no villains, only inevitable frustration. The characters, who
never wish ill for another, act at constant cross purposes, motivated
both by selfish desires and by concern for others, but in all cases
aching for the happiness that Hardy feels everyone deserves. Natural
forces and animals only express the requirements for survival of their
own being. According to Hardy, the "unfulfilledness" of intention is
innate in the condition of any power; that is, even the Intention is
potentially benevolent, but because it cannot fulfill its efforts, its
effect is crippling. Society — the human parallel to the matrix of non-
human interaction, and the central force in *The Woodlanders* and
the two subsequent tragic novels — also behaves according to the only
standard it possesses: an inherent condition of the group-forming
instinct is to restrict individual will.

# I

But preparations for tragedy do not guarantee the utilization of materials in a conventional tragic manner. The lack of a central character or action in the presentation of the great natural law of Unfulfilled

Intention prevents *The Woodlanders* from satisfying traditional assumptions and expectations concerning intensity and the focus of aesthetic energy in a tragedy. Henchard in *The Mayor of Casterbridge* is a narrow-minded grasper of possessions and persons, but he is also strong enough to bear the fate that he fully and humanly draws upon himself. Tess's virtue cannot survive in her world, which will not countenance her sensuality and impetuosity, but she exemplifies an ideal purity that forces a reevaluation of the world's standards of judgment. Even *Far from the Madding Crowd* presents its relationships in such tightly structured movements that they either center in Bathsheba Everdene or, like Fanny Robin's alliance with Sergeant Troy, directly concern her. But in *The Woodlanders,* structural emphasis falls upon all the main characters in too nearly equal a degree to foster the traditional attention to individual fate; that is, structural methods of characterization are the major buttress for Hardy's deliberate announcement that the entire Hintock area is the locus for a tragic expression. Some of these techniques limit the representativeness of the characters; others simply prevent reader attention from settling upon a single character.

The two characters, Giles and Grace, whose fates are the most crucial in the creation of a sense of the difficulty of combating great forces, are chary of exerting will; thus, neither is able to build and maintain a tragic tension. Giles's very being is closely associated with the rural scene of the story; but he has not only awareness and patience before the beginning of the action but also acceptance. There is resolute endurance in his character, but no impetus to struggle. He has a measure of cynicism, it is true, but less so after the English serialization;[7] his primary qualities are a stolid sense of self that prohibits him from imposing his wishes on anyone else, and an aura of stability and strength. His strength supports his passivity and his independence of need. At his first appearance he is resigned to the loss of Grace, and he develops in the course of the novel very little desire to assert his will against the conditions he would have to alter in order to gain happiness with Grace. He evinces practically no inclination to question the suitability of things. Indeed, to Marty's comment that newly planted trees sigh as if "they are very sorry to begin life in earnest — just as we be," Giles remarks critically, "You ought not to feel like that, Marty" (p. 73).

His one deviation from acceptance, his one act of assertion against the conditions of his existence—that is, kissing Grace when he knows that she cannot divorce Fitzpiers and thus is irretrievably lost to him—does not lead to heroic knowledge, for his sense of the strength of the temptation and of the dreadfulness of the act only reinforces his subservience to those imposed conditions, which Hardy portrays in appropriately homely terms: "customs" (p. 333) and "household laws." "The wrong, the social sin, of now taking advantage of the offer of her lips, had a magnitude in the eyes of one whose life had been so primitive, so ruled by household laws as Giles's, which can hardly be explained" (p. 350). His obeisance to this rigid social law contradicts the mythic qualities and natural sources of Giles's strength and thus makes ambivalent his symbolic stature. His basic contradiction is revealed when he is torn by a sense of social sin for having kissed Grace. Giles is a "nature" god (pp. 246-47, 335) rather than a defender of society; and *The Woodlanders* presents a conflict between the courses of natural love and the restraints that an elaborate social code places on the expression and fulfillment of love. Rather than dying for a besieged and doomed traditional system of ethics, in which emotional relationships are based on affinities and on an acceptance of sexual instincts and drives, Giles is forced into the position of sacrificing himself for a precept in a temporal value-system.[8] His death is pitiable and pathetic because he is a physically strong man made physically helpless; but because he never challenges—indeed never comprehends—the forces that destroy him, his death is not tragic.

Moreover, no one who examined the development of the plot could believe that Giles is more important to the novel than Grace is. Grace not only contains within herself the Hardyan division between sophistication and rustic simplicity but her struggles to reconcile that division also give the various subplots their essential relevance. Still, Grace has practically no intentions of her own, and very few inclinations, before Fitzpiers's running off with Felice finally invokes in her an emotional revulsion toward her husband (which is not lasting). At the beginning of the novel she is as willing to marry Giles as not: she feels obliged because of the long understanding between them, but she acquiesces when Melbury demands that she give up Giles in favor of marrying into the social level she had been educated with. Until the final portion of the book, Melbury controls her thoughts and actions; despite her uneasiness "at being the social hope of the family," her father's arguments of a higher social environment influence her (p. 102). At Melbury's later behests she encourages Giles to kiss her; after she learns that a divorce from Fitzpiers is impossible to obtain, it is for her father that she feels the most sorry (p. 354), not for herself or for Giles, for whose feelings throughout the novel she shows the blithest indifference.

It is true that there is in Grace a personal and moral growth, which is identified by her suspicion that her marriage had been a mistake and that "acquiescence in her father's wishes had been degradation to herself" (p. 251). This sort of self-chastening insight leads her to run away despite her father's insistence that she again accept Fitzpiers as her husband. And previous to her flight, Grace's new regard for Giles's rustic virtues, together with her initially languid acceptance of Fitzpiers's affair with Felice, indicate the unity and thoroughness of her development. Youthful feelings had accreted to experience and reflection: "She had looked into her heart, and found that her early interest in Giles Winterborne had become revitalized into growth by her widening perceptions of what was great and little in life" (p. 264). The climax to this growth unquestionably occurs during her desperate flight from her father's home when Fitzpiers returns from the Continent to reclaim her. During her second night in Giles's hut she realizes he is ill outside in the rain, and she calls to him: "*Come to me, dearest! I don't mind what they say or what they think of us any more*" (p. 374).

But Grace's moral maturation is of uncertain durability.[9] She remains in the hut during the day rather than search for Giles, who she suspects is ill, because she fears a passerby may see her and misinterpret her presence with Giles in the isolated area where his hut is located; and her defiance of "what people think" is short-lived. Following Giles's death, she cannot bear to have Melbury "think the utmost" about the appearance of her being found in Giles's hut, and she rebels only briefly against Melbury's plea that she "escape any sound of shame" by telling no one she had lived for several days in Giles's hut and had been with him when he died (pp. 375, 391-92). Grace's deepened perception of Giles's nobility decays with time; she returns to her husband against her better judgment, after she has realized that no divine law binds her to him (p. 370), and even after she has begun to question the validity of the religious ritual that had united them (p. 428). What Hardy presents in the denouement of Grace's "development" is, then, the antithesis of tragedy in its un-raveling of a personal growth based on experience and in its repudia-tion of morally beneficial suffering that had led to insight both per-sonal and universal. The aesthetic-moral experience of *The Wood-landers* suggests a pervasive hopelessness based upon the shallow-ness of the individual when faced with basic drives. It is not Grace's conscious volition or any extension of acquired quality stemming from experience that brings about the reunion with her husband. It is the animal quality of sexual need, indicated by the excitement en-gendered in her during their nocturnal rendezvous and the incident with the man-trap. To help clarify the sexual nature of Grace's bond-age to Fitzpiers, Hardy added Melbury's last speech to post-first edi-tion texts of the novel: "Let her take him back to her bed if she will!" (p. 439).

The structural complexities in the novel's tragic characteri-zations are amplified by Melbury's role. The only major character who does not experience romantic love in the course of a novel based on love relationships, he is still the most traditionally suitable tragic character. He is fully as sympathetic as Giles, and he as well as Grace reacts confusedly and self-betrayingly to the sophistication encroach-ing upon Wessex, the world of primitive and accurate communion with nature. Next to Marty and Giles, Melbury comes nearest to knowing "the tongue of the trees and fruits and flowers themselves" (p. 400); and his position as a wealthy lumber trader, which he has gained by his own efforts (p. 33), and as the descendant of an old Hintock family (pp. 132, 192), is proof of his control of and his au-thority in his universe. But in his ambitions for his daughter, he be-comes false to his better personal feelings, and more significantly in this novel, to the values of his universe. With a countryman's awe for family name and rank, and a self-made man's awe for unearned social position, Melbury's vanity and boundless love for his daughter inspire him to overstep tradition and to challenge the class system, because, ironically, he is unaware that his family is as good as Fitzpiers's.

Melbury is the cause of much of the action in *The Woodlanders*, dating from his scheme to marry his daughter Grace to Giles as a way of making amends for having years earlier won away from Giles's father the affections of the young girl who became Grace's mother, and then from his violation of his scheme in encouraging Grace to marry Fitzpiers. Melbury can face up to the results of his subverting the plan that Grace and Giles marry; he accepts, perhaps unreasonably, the full responsibility for Grace's unhappiness with the unfaithful Fitzpiers (p. 257). He continually reevaluates his efforts, coming at one point to a near-total alienation from the rural certitudes of his life: he feels he has lost his ability "to form a conjecture on the weather, or the time, or the fruit-promise, so great was his self-mistrust" (p. 270). Nonetheless, he continues to meddle rashly, bringing about the elopement of Grace's husband with Mrs. Charmond and encouraging Grace and Giles to resume their old affection for each other, even before he has seen the London lawyer about the possibility of a divorce for Grace. Only after his last intervention into someone else's life — his refusal to support Grace's desire not to return to the man who had deserted her — brings about Grace's unconventional flight and Giles's death does Melbury cease offering advice. Through painful experience he becomes able not only to let his daughter live her life but to have insight into others' characters as well. In his last speech, he expresses recognition both of the sexual basis for Grace's return to Fitzpiers and of the transient quality of Fitzpiers's faithfulness, which together will produce for his daughter an unsatisfactory life:

> "Well — he's her husband," Melbury said to himself, "and let her take him back to her bed if she will! . . . But let her bear in mind that the woman walks and laughs somewhere at this very moment whose neck he'll be coling [embracing] next year as he does hers to-night; and as he did Felice Charmond's last year; and Suke Damson's the year afore! . . . It's a forlorn hope for her; and God knows how it will end!" [Pp. 439-40]

But no matter how satisfactorily Melbury may perform the suffering and educative functions of the tragic hero, the novel's central sufferers are his daughter and her woodland lover, Giles. Despite his representing a traditional society's suicidal pandering to false values, Melbury's mental suffering and sense of guilt for his misguided am-

bitions do not overshadow the more compelling agonies of temptation and resignation undergone by Giles, nor the more intense
discord between self and society that Grace suffers as the embodi-
ment of conflicting modes of existence.

Thus, attempting to equate the characters who perform in the
most conventional tragic manner with those who are central to the
plot leads one into qualifications that *ipso facto* broaden the usual
concepts of the tragic hero. To put forth either Fitzpiers or Felice as
the central figure would distort the novel, even though both have
basically good intentions that are thwarted by forces in their lives
which they cannot withstand, and though both learn something about
themselves in the course of their experiences. Neither makes the
attempt to withstand which could make their capitulation to destructive impulses meaningful by itself. And Marty, however attractive and
sympathetic a figure, neither grows nor learns through her suffering.
Hardy notes in his last view of her that she has almost been abstracted
beyond the plane of educative suffering:

> As this solitary and silent girl stood there in the moonlight, a straight
> slim figure, clothed in a plaitless gown, the contours of womanhood so
> undeveloped as to be scarcely perceptible in her, the marks of poverty
> and toil effaced by the misty hour, she touched sublimity at points, and
> looked almost like a being who had rejected with indifference the attri-
> bute of sex for the loftier quality of abstract humanism. [P. 443]

Marty is indeed the fit moral companion for the stalwart Winterborne. She incarnates the strength of Hardy's peasant stock, who feel
deeply but quietly, accepting stoically whatever fate gives them. But
since she never experiences even the possibility of choice, she cannot
perform calamitous and willful error.

A complex employment of point of view contributes toward
preventing a single figure from attaining central importance in the
novel. *The Woodlanders* is told from a point of view that can best be
described as controlled by an omniscient author who employs both
his oracular stance and a multiplicity of limited perspectives. The
reader's interest does not focus throughout on one character, as it
does with only incidental exceptions on Tess or Jude Fawley, or as it
does on Henchard in *The Mayor of Casterbridge*. Several characters
combine strengths and weaknesses to make them important figures.

The omniscient author permits each character to provide at least once the perspective for certain events, and the perspective moves irregularly from one character to another. After the opening scene in *The Woodlanders,* for example, the narrative perspective shifts from Marty to Melbury to Giles to Grace to Giles to Fitzpiers to Grace to Fitzpiers — and by this time we are only at Fitzpiers's first visit to Felice; the shifting of perspective continues. No single character is examined in such detail or depth or at such length as to make his or her internal struggles synthetize those of the other characters and therefore to raise him or her into the position of the hero.

Equally pertinent is that the center of narration of this novel at any given place may not be the character whose fate is being worked out at the particular time. The most telling use of this structural device occurs when Melbury provides the narrative perspective as he discovers for himself and interprets for the reader the progress of Fitzpiers's affair with Felice (pp. 257-309). Because someone outside the affair describes it, the importance of the character of its perpetrators contracts at a time when in a conventional narrative it should expand in complexity. We never are made to feel the tensions of Fitzpiers and Felice's desire, Felice's helpless sense of shame, and Fitzpiers's frustrated social ambitions. We do not even know whether Fitzpier's ill-fated nocturnal visit to Felice is prompted by humanitarian feelings of a doctor at the news of a patient's ill-ease or by romantic desire for one last meeting with his mistress before she departs for the Continent. This use of point of view also has the effect of elevating Melbury to a high position in the novel's structure. In one respect he deserves this emphasis, since it is his ambition that determines Grace's fate; but the primary interests at this stage of the story are not Melbury or his societal role but the true nature of Fitzpiers and Felice's affair and the effect that the affair has upon Grace's ambivalent feelings.

The place given to Giles and Marty in the plot further prevents a conventional tragic focus. Although the sole character who demonstrates true physical heroism and stoic endurance of unwonted suffering, Giles appears only intermittently throughout the book, and he disappears entirely for the long middle span of Grace's courtship and marriage and Fitzpiers's dalliance with Mrs. Charmond. Marty is Giles's true partner in knowing nature, and she as much as he personifies the quality of a moral system against the background of which tragedy can be enacted. She flits briefly in and out of the plot, mainly by authorial references to Mrs. Charmond wearing the wig made from her hair. She affects the plot only twice (writing on Giles's wall and sending a letter to Fitzpiers) and then only to precipitate actions that would have occurred without her; and she concludes the novel with a paean to the memory of the fallen Giles. Marty is at the moral and thematic center of the novel, but she is as nearly irrelevant to the plot as a major character can conceivably be.

Hardy's manipulation of the center of interest permits the reader to identify in turn with a number of characters and thus to base perceptions upon a broadness of understanding. Hardy prohibits over-facile judgments on blame and causation, and forces the reader to hold his attitudes in suspension. The different judgments upon Fitz-piers that are possible illustrate how this roving perspective affects a single controversial character. Through the villagers' opening comments we expect a grasper of knowledge and a philosopher while we discount their naive appellation of Fitzpiers as "devil's man." From the viewpoint of Giles at old South's bedside we see Fitzpiers as a socially snobbish and indifferent doctor, callous alike to mental disorder and death. As the story progresses, other sides of Fitzpiers's flashy shallowness become evident: he sleeps of mornings, reads French novels in preference to science manuals and philosophic tomes, indolently switches subjects of study before he can become deeply involved in any, wishes half-seriously (but mostly petulantly) that his wife would die, and does not deign to apologize to his wife for his infidelities. But the stronger side of Fitzpiers also constantly receives attention: he is genuinely intelligent, he takes the initiative in love, he does not pretend to hold a sanguine attitude toward the duration of love in order to attract either Grace or Felice, and he is often considerate toward Grace. Hardy gives Fitzpiers qualities that would be admired in Giles as strength; indeed, Hardy seems to admire them in Fitzpiers as basic honesty. Felice's characterization could also be cited in detail, as could Grace's, Melbury's, and to some degree Giles's, but what has been said of Fitzpiers's adequately demonstrates the care Hardy took to balance qualities in his characterizations. The creation of ambivalent attitudes toward a number of characters directly promotes the effect of *The Woodlanders* as a tragedy.

# II

Those who have questioned Hardy's development of a tragic theme in *The Woodlanders* have usually measured the novel against conventional tragic theories,[10] and according to those tests, their negative reactions are quite justifiable. But Hardy was not trying to write a conventional tragedy; what he did write is as complex and admirable in its utilization of materials in a particular way as, say, *The Mayor of Casterbridge*, which, John Paterson has pointed out, is a superbly çoordinated mustering of traditional tragic echoes and shadowing.[11] The limitations of *The Woodlanders* as a conventional tragedy, which I have been sketching, implicitly elucidate the structural principle that controls the organization of the novel.

The rationale for the form of *The Woodlanders* lies deep in Hardy's attitudes. He was at odds with the way of life he saw developing around him. Perceptive, sensitive, and disciplined in an environment where feelings and intuitions provided standards of value, he came to intellectual and emotional maturity in a rapidly expanding industrial society. Widespread disregard for humanistic values was buttressed by economic theorizing of *laissez faire* and the scientific generalizations of Lyell, Darwin, and Huxley in which feelings and human will, if indeed they existed at all in a conditioned empirical universe, had little practical efficacy. The world of rural Dorset which he loved was eroding under the combined tides of increased communication and transportation and the tornado of financial imperatives that made the settled modes of agricultural and community traditions impossible to retain. As with most romantics who are too aware of realistic activities to accept a palliative justification for life, disillusionment raised in Hardy a discontent with what seemed to be the causes for the unsatisfactory conditions of existence and the imbalance between what ought to have been and what were the possibilities of achieving happiness. In his earlier novels Hardy had presented character as one cause of man's tragic plight and inevitable destruction ("Character is Fate, says Novalis" in *The Mayor of Casterbridge* is the most succinct statement of the bias underlying this analysis); alternately, he blamed the incomprehensible and uncomprehending supernatural forces that are symbolized by implacable natural phenomena such as Egdon Heath or the distant stars in *Two on a Tower.* But neither force by itself seemed an adequate explanation for the peculiar varieties of man's misery. Hardy's belief that individually man is sincere in his willingness to foster the happiness of his fellowman obviates the first force as the primary cause of others' unhappiness. And if, as Hardy felt, the great natural forces affecting life are unconsciously and aimlessly exercising their influences, it is contradictory and fruitless to attack the seeming malignity with which man's efforts are frustrated by these forces. When he came to write *The Woodlanders,* Hardy was ready to analyze in greater subtlety than before another possible agency, society, which being conscious could be malign, and being aggregate could be unable to tolerate individual avenues to happiness which challenge the security of avenues suitable to the community as a whole.

Though the effects of social pressures on individual choice appear in earlier novels — witness Thomasin's marriage to Wildeve and Viviette's to the Bishop (in *Two on a Tower*) — in *The Woodlanders* there is a marked increase in emphasis upon society's effort to vitiate natural impulse. Hardy explores this subject in greater detail than in his previous novels through the use of a structure that is essentially new. Instead of presenting one or two characters and implying by extension of statement the universality of their problem, he presents a number of characters from a spectrum of social and economic classes who face the common problem of reconciling their personal iconoclastic desires with the demands of their society. He does not, of course, completely shunt aside all aspects of the previously examined forces in developing his new vision. Hardy, I have noted above, brings nature as well as society into his indictment, because the impulses affecting one element in man's situation also affect the other, a concept that he demonstrates by giving human qualities to animals and to insensate forces of nature. Nonetheless, by portraying nature as suffering along with man, he qualifies the complicity of natural forces. He also throws into the amalgam of social and natural restrictions an almost metaphysical agent that helps to limit the range of options among which free will may operate; in a passage describing the tension at the Melburys's after Giles's clumsy Christmas party, Hardy remarks that "the petulance that relatives show towards each other is in truth directed against that intangible Cause which has shaped the situation no less for the offenders than the offended" (p. 95).

Still, as Hardy implies in his 1895 preface, it is the body of accreted traditions by which sexual relationships are maintained and regulated that is the principal determinant of unhappiness in *The Woodlanders:*

> In the present novel, as in one or two others of this series which involve the question of matrimonial divergence, the immortal puzzle—given the man and woman, how to find a basis for their sexual relation—is left it where it stood; and it is tacitly assumed for the purposes of the story that no doubt of the depravity of the erratic heart who feels some second person to be better suited to his or her tastes than the one with whom he has contracted to live, enters the head of reader or writer for a moment. From the point of view of marriage as a distinct covenant or undertaking, decided on by two people fully cognizant of all its possible issues, and competent to carry them through, this assumption is, of course, logical. Yet no thinking person supposes that, on the broader ground of how to afford the greatest happiness to the units of human society during their brief transit through this sorry world, there is no more to be said on this covenant: and it is certainly not supposed by the writer of these pages. But, as Gibbon blandly remarks on the evidence for and against Christian miracles, "the duty of an historian does not call upon him to interpose his private judgment in this nice and important controversy."[Pp. vii-viii]

Felice Charmond protests to Fitzpiers against the rigidity of conventional emotional releases: "O! why were we given hungry hearts and wild desires if we have to live in a world like this?" (p. 237). Grace, unconscious of her own sexual drives, does not echo Felice's appeal. She rebels more significantly. Her awareness of the irrevocable damage that socially admirable behavior can cause is sharply directed against the incongruity of public morality, when it finally dawns on her that Giles is desperately ill outside the hut: "How selfishly correct I am always—too, too correct! Can it be that cruel propriety is killing the dearest heart that ever woman clasped to her own!" (p. 378).

The basis for evaluating propriety in *The Woodlanders* is both religious and social, but primarily social. After Fitzpiers's infidelity Grace denies that she is "bound to him by any divine law" although she determines to obey her vow (p. 370). Grace's dilemma in being married to Fitzpiers is interpreted by Melbury and Giles as social, not religious. Melbury after he perceives that something is drastically wrong in his daughter's marriage questions the justice of the custom "that a woman once given to a man for life took, as a rule, her lot as it came, and made the best of it, without external interference" (p. 260), and later presses determinedly and swiftly for the divorce without questioning the distinction between religious and civil grounds for divorce. Giles too dwells primarily on the social ramifications of the proposed divorce. His feelings upon hearing about it are those of bemused disbelief. "Surely the adamantine barrier of marriage with another could not be pierced like this! It did violence to custom. Yet a new law might do anything" (p. 333). The guilt that Giles feels in kissing Grace stems from social and domestic violations, not religious, even though the extent of violation in his eyes is enough to demand the final reparation. A final passage demonstrating this point occurs in Grace's musing over the marriage service before her last rendezvous with her estranged husband. The sentence, "She wondered whether God really did join them together" (p. 428), is an addition in the manuscript.[12] It is a jarring addition, and its meaning is somewhat obscure in context; but in weakening the religious sanction of marriage its connotation is obvious. If God did not join Fitzpiers and her together, and if they are therefore not responsible to God for the permanence of their union, then society and its "household laws" become responsible for the restrictive conditions of marriage.

In this novel, then, in which the fate of all characters is equally dependent on socially acceptable modes of sexual deportment, Hardy has avoided concentrating aesthetic attention upon one consciousness or upon the fate of one character. Whether individually guilty or innocent of "illicit" sexual or social ambitions, the characters are tragically destroyed by the effects of society's rigidity; through the number of and resemblances among the struggles rather than through profound ramifications drawn from a single struggle, the fates of the characters are expanded into universal applicability. Instead of one character serving as the symbol or representative of mankind as in the conventional tragedy, in *The Woodlanders* one sort of social force serves as the symbol or representative of the oppressiveness of society as a whole.

The effects of these techniques broaden the import of the scheme of tangled human doings. By compounding the disasters and decentralizing the reader's concern, Hardy brings the reader into a richly varied identification with the milieu and actors of the drama. In *The Mayor of Casterbridge,* one powerful figure attracts the deepest sympathy of a certain part of the reader's psyche, whereas in *The Woodlanders* a multiple of more complex if less individually profound characters engross the reader at a number of levels. Spanning a great part of the continuum of benevolence and self-centeredness, of aspirations and attainments, of exertion and failure, these levels subsume each human being, who is neither good nor evil altogether but is ambivalently motivated with contradictory impulses. *The Woodlanders* does not stimulate one into recognizing, at the height of aesthetic perception, his kinship with the heroic man; *The Woodlanders* persuades one at a rational and reflective level that in his compound of strengths and weaknesses he is kin to all humanity struggling against psychological and social forces similar to those he can sense in his own life. Each character of *The Woodlanders* represents an aspect of the totality of lives affected by social forces. The representation is not exhaustive, nor could it be in fiction; but a narrative involving five people of various virtues and failings at cross purposes with each other and frequently at cross purposes within themselves, and unable both to communicate love and to adhere to social demands, richly embodies the human situation. Hardy's consistent portrayal of the inability of men to realign personal intention with the "intentions"—that is, predilections—of society vivifies the dilemma.

    *The Woodlanders* is the most pessimistic of the Wessex novels. Two modes of society—as an aggregate of customs and expectations and as a collection of independently acting individuals—conspire to frustrate and overthrow human efforts aimed at happiness. In most of the earlier novels, human companionship can alleviate suffering, or, as in the darker portions of *Tess of the d'Urbervilles* and in *Jude the Obscure,* humanity is so obviously malign and untrustworthy that no one would dream of placing trust in it. But in *The Woodlanders,* where society provides the *modus vivendi* of conduct, trust is placed in individual components—and discovered to have been misplaced. As Melbury learns in Hintock House, even the fairest exterior and the most genteel surroundings give no assurance of basic decency (p. 302). Grace's observation, made as she watches Fitzpiers ride "through the gorgeous autumn landscape" on his way to visit Mrs.

Charmond at Middleton Abbey — " In all this proud show some kernels were unsound as her own situation" (p. 245) — further sets forth the individual's problem of ascertaining truth. Conventional appearances do not reflect reality; they provide no sound basis for judgments that are necessary for the conduct of life. *Jude the Obscure* distresses because its view of life is often bitter and oppressive, but the bitterness and oppressiveness permit one to react to the novel as a distortion or intensification of actual conditions of life. *The Woodlanders* catches one unaware, since the superficial impression is one of calm reflection existing in a woodlands retreat disturbed only by relatively mild fluctuations of romantic love. But along with the external beauty of landscape and the delicacy and toleration of individual personality, the novel presents an interpretation of such pervasive frustration that the inevitable miscalculations within human relationships and the constrictions of rigid social decrees can be approximated only by images of bleeding tree trunks and predatory animals.

# 6

## TESS OF THE D'URBERVILLES:

### *Pure Tragedy of Consciousness*

The formal principles of the novels before *Tess of the d'Urbervilles* can be thought of as at once proportional and spatial; that is, they help to determine emphases within the material as the plot progresses, and they imply that significance is at least partially external to the individual. Most clearly in *Far from the Madding Crowd* and *The Return of the Native,* those principles literally define the balance and stress of passages of character delineation and such matters as the symbolic value of geographic placement on the verge or in the center of Egdon Heath. The cyclic pattern underlying *The Mayor of Casterbridge* encompasses the progression of the plot as well as the spatial and temporal conditions of the tragic situation, and although in a considerably more abstract manner, so does the idea of universal tragic stature in *The Woodlanders,* as characters alternate in assuming and abandoning the center of attention.

In his last two great novels, which have been most keenly etched in readers' memories as uniquely Hardyan stories (though not all readers admire them equally), the primary formal principles are neither spatial nor proportional. The stories do have spatial schemes, based essentially on the reenactment of similar experiences, which take place in localities of special interrelationships. But in the uniqueness of the novels those spatial schemes are more or less incidental, caused primarily by the necessity for plot and for movement among the characters.

The important formal principles of the late novels are concepts of consciousness — concepts of the manner in which perception of experience shapes the meaning of the experience and, indeed, even constitutes its significance. These principles reflect the Manichean bias of Hardy's philosophical metaphors and his lifelong interest in the duality of the apparent and the real. They are also the natural development from the principles we have examined in the previous novels. The development can perhaps be most readily traced from *The Mayor of Casterbridge* and *The Woodlanders* to *Tess of the d'Urbervilles* — from a position of externality providing significance for the individual (Henchard) to a position of rich but ambiguous individuality-dissolving experience (*The Woodlanders*) to a position in which significance is caused solely by the internal qualities of the subject (Tess). The development continues to *Jude the Obscure,* which offers another consciousness — one not directly involved in the action, that of the narrator — interleaving in a highly complex manner interpretations of reality with those of the protagonist. The abstract formal principles are of course not entirely without previous manifestations in Hardy's work. In *Far from the Madding Crowd* he defines as of the utmost importance in tragic effect the ability of the character for sustained and intense suffering; and in most of his novels the narrator expresses opinions. But it was only after *The Woodlanders* that the abstractions took precedence over concepts of form that include spatial organization. Moreover, his final vision of significance has few points of contact with the prescriptions and restrictions of classical tragic theory. He did not explicitly reject classical theories or examples after *The Woodlanders* — he used the idea of the family curse in both *Tess of the d'Urbervilles* and *Jude the Obscure* — but his sense of the tragic was not confined to characters or dilemmas of classical "correct" dimensions.

*Tess of the d'Urbervilles* stresses the subjectivity of experience and judgment. In basing the aesthetic effect of his work upon the principle of subjectivity, Hardy broadened a trail rather than blazed one, although I know of no earlier fictional tragedy to employ the concept.[1] The aesthetic energy in subjectiveness was bizarrely thrust upon Western consciousness by Rousseau, especially in his *Confes-*

*sions,* and its fecundity is still evident. Keats's odes and Wordworth's *The Prelude,* and such later works as Conrad's and Faulkner's novels, are well known examples of the capacity of the mind to make its own self-significating world. Hardy shares an essentially romantic perception with these writers, but less sophisticated. Although an awareness of the principle is clear in all of his work — I have already remarked upon its appearance in *The Return of the Native* — the full exploitation of subjectivity as an index to tragedy appears first in *Tess of the d'Urbervilles.* It is perhaps partly because tragedy was not an active form during the era of the aggrandizement of common humanity by romanticism (though it does appear in the subgenre of Gothicism in both fiction and drama) that Hardy was the first to structure a tragedy upon the individual's comprehension of himself rather than upon his relation to a social world; Conrad's *Lord Jim* also considers the validity of this principle, but ultimately rejects anarchical individualism.[2] (It could be argued that Ibsen, whose works inspired Hardy to use socially lower-class protagonists and unconventional themes, had given Hardy direction in the matter of subjectivity as well. But Ibsen's protagonists, although remarkably egoistic and thus in this special sense "subjective," are essentially imperceptive.)

Each of Hardy's tragedies is in its own way a brief for the desirability of individual freedom, but in *Tess of the d'Urbervilles* he expands freedom of conscience to include freedom of consciousness, a near anarchy of perception. "The world is only a psychological phenomenon," says Hardy-as-narrator early in the novel (p. 108); and he demonstrates in a variety of ways within the novel the impossibility of objective and detached observation and evaluation of life. The meaning of an action depends not only upon the situation, which in itself is probably unique, but also upon the beholders, who while broadly consistent in their characterizations are not constant. (Angel's declaration to Tess, following her story of her past, that she is not the woman he married earlier in the day; Tess's later decision that after marrying Angel she was a different person from the one she had been with Alec — these declarations reflect the evanescence of life as surely as they do Tess's and Angel's confusion about morality and their own evolving personalities.)

The emphasis upon subjectivity of experience locates the

source of the tragic emotion in *Tess of the d'Urbervilles* within the
human consciousness rather than within some sort of relationship
between the individual and environment, or between individuals, or
between an individual and the moral order of his world. Obviously,
there are social and interpersonal relationships, and Hardy does not
fail to show how they impinge upon and affect the consciousness of
the separate individual. But the tragic emotion itself is subjective,
centering in characters essentially isolated within selves that do not
remain stable entities even within themselves.[3]  All tragedies are in
differing degrees tragedies of the individual. Antigone may represent
a way of confronting arbitrary authority, but she is also a person who
suffers and dies in the flesh. Willy Loman may represent a segment
of an economic community who cannot distinguish between practical
reality and the ideals of the community, but he is also an individual
who drives his car into a bridge abutment so that his son Biff can start
his life anew with the twenty thousand dollars from the insurance
policy. *Tess of the d'Urbervilles* is a tragedy of the individual, by
which I mean that there is no valid way to judge Tess according to an
external standard of social necessity or duty. Because the novel lacks
a clear moral imperative, the logic of aesthetics requires that Tess's
primary duty, if such a moralistic word can be used in the context of
this story, is to her own state of mind. Here only the consciousness
of the individual offers the means of evaluation and then only for a
moment. In that the individual's egocentricity is reinforced by this
basic premise of the novel's structure, any judgment imposed by a
conglomeration of non-selves is irrelevant, beside the point. Within
this sort of aesthetic environ, tragedy arises when the impetus of one's
consciousness cannot be practically realized by the individual, or
when efforts to achieve realization result in the frustration or destruction of the individual's true self (see *Early Life,* p. 230, for Hardy's definition of this sort of tragedy). To describe tragedy in this way
is, partially, another way to describe the tragic outcome of conflict
between an individual and the external world. Hardy's expression of
subjectivity is, after all, only an explicit enlargement in a structural
context of a quality of tragedy that is universal. The tragedy of individual consciousness as manifested in *Tess of the d'Urbervilles* is
unique largely in the extent to which Hardy withholds the grounds
for interpretation of judgment. Although outside forces can frustrate

one's consciousness, they cannot be trusted as an index to measure either the superiority or inferiority of the moral quality of the consciousness that is being frustrated. Thus, even the narrator cannot be assumed to offer a permanently stable perspective,[4] although paradoxically it is the narrator's tone and turns of phrase that serve frequently to remind us of the limitations of the perspectives of the separate characters. (In *Antigone,* on the other hand, the social principle of obedience to the king—which is imperative for political stability—is confronted with Antigone's sense of religious and familial duty. The Western inclination to prefer Antigone's justification to Creon's countermands the play's subtlety in presenting balanced alternatives and ignores a historical context that emphasizes social responsibility. There are only two moral poles in *Antigone,* both eloquently defined and largely unchanging; in *Tess of the d'Urbervilles* all is flux, and moral positions appear to have only temporary validity. Tragedy occurs because Tess's character is hard-pressed by her past, the circumstances of her present, and her rejection by society and Angel. Hardy intimates, however, that society's reasons for rejecting Tess are not necessarily entirely wrong nor evil. Indeed, neither the regenerated Angel nor the unsparingly besieged Tess categorically and permanently denies the validity of conventional views of chastity. The problem, as Angel comes to see in Brazil, is precisely that society makes no provision for a special case like Tess's, whose justifications rely upon the unique self (p. 435).

Hardy establishes subjectivity as the basis of perceiving the novel's action through a variety of methods, whose effect is to turn the individual upon himself for judgments and to deny the usefulness and trustworthiness of external perceptions and moralities. One method is to state explicitly that the individual creates his own world, that this view of the world may be in accord neither with pre-conceptions based on conventions nor with other people's views. In stating that the world is only a psychological phenomenon, Hardy employs the concept of correspondence that is frequent in his works:

> [Tess's] flexuous and stealthy figure became an integral part of the scene. At times her whimsical fancy would intensify natural processes around her till they *seemed* a part of her own story. Rather they *became* a part of it; for the world is only a psychological phenomenon, and what

they *seemed* they *were.* The midnight airs and gusts, moaning amongst the tightly-wrapped buds and bark of the winter twigs, were formulae of bitter reproach. A wet day was the expression of irremediable grief at her weakness in the mind of some vague ethical being whom she could not class definitely as the God of her childhood, and could not comprehend as any other.

But this encompassment of her own characterization, based on shreds of convention, peopled by phantoms and voices antipathetic to her, was a sorry and mistaken creation of Tess's fancy—a cloud of moral hobgoblins by which she was terrified without reason. It was they that were out of harmony with the actual world, not she. Walking among the sleeping birds in the hedges, watching the skipping rabbits on a moonlit warren, or standing under a pheasant-laden bough, she looked upon herself as a figure of Guilt intruding into the haunts of Innocence. But all the while she was making a distinction where there was no difference. Feeling herself in antagonism she was quite in accord. She had been made to break an accepted social law, but no law known to the environment in which she fancied herself such an anomaly. [P. 108; my italics]

The second paragraph makes evident that the perspective of the individual's consciousness is not always accurate. Indeed, as David Lodge points out, in Hardy's own terms ("the world is only a psychological phenomenon"), "the view expressed in the second paragraph is as 'subjective' as that expressed in the first, and has no greater validity."[5] Hardy soon makes clear, however, that Tess's consciousness has more potential for growth than has convention, the source of Tess's "bitter [self-] reproach." Tess becomes aware that her view of condemnatory nature has been shortsighted. The combination of common sense and fatalism informs her that "the past was past" and that in a few years the actors in her drama would be "as if they had never been, and she herself grassed down and forgotten. Meanwhile the trees were just as green as before; the birds sang and the sun shone as clearly now as ever. The familiar surroundings had not darkened because of her grief, nor sickened because of her pain" (p. 115).

Accompanying and substantiating Tess's changes in view about life are further observations about the subjectivity of life and the inadequacy of convention to provide a foundation for judgment in personal matters.

She might have seen that what had bowed her head so profoundly—

the thought of the world's concern at her situation — was founded on an illusion. She was not an existence, an experience, a passion, a structure of sensations, to anybody but herself. To all humankind besides Tess was only a passing thought....Most of the misery [at being an unwed mother] had been generated by her conventional aspect, and not by her innate sensations. [P. 115]

This passage, as clearly as any that can be used to elucidate Hardy's interest in consciousness, stresses the isolation of the individual, his separation from the consciousness of the people around him, his lack of importance to his peers and environment. Hardy, by deflating the social significance of the individual, is obviously shifting the idea of tragedy away from one that assumes the existence of an externally signifying figure to one that assumes each figure "signifies" only to himself. The idea expressed the unique quality of tragedy in *Tess of the d'Urbervilles*, that is, within the pages of the novel Tess is tragic only to herself. To others, she is a puzzling daughter, a temptingly lovely girl and woman, an image of purity, a fallen woman. None of these descriptions approximates what Oedipus is to his society nor what Blanche and Joe Christmas are to their respective milieus and associates, although the feature of "special meanings" of the individual has interesting parallels in Arthur Miller's Willy Loman.

Tess's mental states determine her actions and her attitudes toward life. These states, moreover, she has some conscious control over. She had partly shared Joan Durbeyfield's ambitions to benefit from their discovered ancestry, but following her seduction by Alec and the birth and death of Sorrow she became resolved on one point: "There should be no more d'Urberville air-castles in the dreams and deeds of her new life" at Talbothays dairy (p. 126). Impelled to go to Talbothays by a "stir of germination," she does not forget that though her life there may be idyllic, there is another and more threatening kind of life. Tess's affection for Angel keeps back "the gloomy spectres that would persist in their attempts to touch her — doubt, fear, moodiness, care, shame. She knew that they were waiting like wolves just outside the circumscribing light, but she had long spells of power to keep them in hungry subjection there" (p. 249). At other times her entire existence is in her subjective life, as when she shuts out the cruelties forced upon her by Angel. Although she goes back to work as a dairy-maid following his departure for Brazil, she takes little

interest in life. "Mentally she remained in utter stagnation, a condition which the mechanical occupation rather fostered than checked.
Her consciousness was at that other dairy, at that other season, in the
presence of the tender lover who had confronted her there— he who,
the moment she had grasped him to keep for her own, had disappeared like a shape in a vision" (p. 347).

To isolate the individual consciousness from value-systems of
its environs as Hardy does in *Tess of the d'Urbervilles* does not in the
least mean that he thinks he is writing anything other than a tragedy.
His description of Angel Clare's discovery that humble life on a dairy
can be as intense as a life lived in more opulent surroundings is similar in its suggestion of universal tragic potentiality to Hardy's comment in *The Woodlanders* that in sequestered spots sometimes
"dramas of a grandeur and unity truly Sophoclean are enacted."
Social distinction is mentioned, but more pertinently Hardy emphasizes again the role that the individual plays in creating the quality
of his own experience:

> Many besides Angel have learnt that the magnitude of lives is not as to
> their external displacements, but as to their subjective experiences. The
> impressionable peasant leads a larger, fuller, more dramatic life than
> the pachydermatous king. Looking at it thus he found that life was to
> be seen of the same magnitude here as elsewhere.
>
> ...Tess was no insignificant creature to toy with and dismiss; but
> a woman living her precious life— a life which, to herself who endured
> or enjoyed it, possessed as great a dimension as the life of the mightiest
> to himself. Upon her sensations the whole world depended to Tess;
> through her existence all her fellow-creatures existed, to her. The uni-
> verse itself only came into being for Tess on the particular day in the
> particular year in which she was born. [Pp. 198-99]

Hardy gives deep attention to Tess; the reaction she consequently
calls forth in the reader stems from the innate and peculiar qualities
he attributes to her as an individual. Even her youthfulness is an ex-
trinsic matter; we react to Tess's sufferings as profoundly as we do
because of the way she herself has reacted to her experiences, not
because of how extensive or prolonged her experiences have been.
"Experience is as to intensity, and not as to duration," Hardy reminds
us (p. 160).[6]

For individual consciousness to have the necessary effect of heightening the context of the novel to a pitch appropriate to tragedy, Hardy must go against a basic generic assumption of fiction, that it is a societal art form within which inheres a comprehension — however vaguely formed and abstract — that there is a correct set of patterns by which the characters' thoughts and behavior can be evaluated. Indeed, the characters' existences in most fiction (with the exception of a fable or allegory) acquire substance in the full, concretized world of the novel by the operation of these patterns. To show Hardy's departure from convention, my discussion takes up what I hope I have already made obvious in my considerations of "the world is only a psychological phenomenon." That is, I wish to discuss the ways in which Hardy announces the internality of stature and stress in *Tess of the d'Urbervilles*. The pervasive subjectiveness of stature and the isolation of individual consciousness are developed by his use of point of view, by animistic scenes, by his emphasis upon the relativity of opinion and perspective, and by a number of features best indicated by the term *mysticism*. Each contributes toward disintegrating the idea that there is a final external truth.

# I

Mystical features are the most direct aspect of the novel which supports the emotional potentiality within the individual, for the basic quality of mysticism is the supremacy of the unique vision, a way of knowing truth that can be reduced into words or images only at the cost of its directness. In other words, a mystical vision can be talked about, or even codified (as in Buddhism); but it cannot be communicated to another consciousness in its original brilliance. The mystic in the ultimate sense is subject only to the inward law, grasped intuitively and perhaps comprehended but fleetingly. Mystical experiences are within Tess's everyday capacity. Tess first attracts Angel's attention by expressing her opinion at a breakfast at Talbothays Dairy that "our souls can be made to go outside our bodies when we are alive" (p. 154); and their first personal conversation occurs when she is deeply affected by Angel's harp-playing one evening shortly after.

The physical setting for their conversation possesses a mystical aura, lending credence to the intensity of Tess's reaction to the music. "It was a typical summer evening in June, the atmosphere being in such delicate equilibrium and so transmissive that inanimate objects seemed endowed with two or three senses, if not five" (p. 157). She is in a receptive frame of mind; for though "to speak absolutely" both Angel's instrument and his execution were poor, "the relative is all," and Tess draws nearer to the player, unseen. She has a nearly classic mystical experience, which climaxes in the last paragraph of the following passage. She loses her awareness of the boundaries of reality; Hardy describes a commingling of the sense perceptions in order to communicate the keenness of intellect and the recomprehension of reality that occur through mystical insight.

There was no distinction between the near and the far, and an auditor felt close to everything within the horizon. The soundlessness impressed her as a positive entity rather than as the mere negation of noise. It was broken by the strumming of strings.

Tess had heard those notes in the attic above her head. Dim, flattened, constrained by their confinement, they had never appealed to her as now, when they wandered in the still air with a stark quality like that of nudity. To speak absolutely, both instrument and execution were poor; but the relative is all, and as she listened Tess, like a fascinated bird, could not leave the spot. Far from leaving she drew up towards the performer, keeping behind the hedge that he might not guess her presence.

The outskirt of the garden in which Tess found herself had been left uncultivated for some years, and was now damp and rank with juicy grass which sent up mists of pollen at a touch; and with tall blooming weeds emitting offensive smells — weeds whose red and yellow and purple hues formed a polychrome as dazzling as that of cultivated flowers. She went stealthily as a cat through this profusion of growth, gathering cuckoo-spittle on her skirts, cracking snails that were underfoot, staining her hands with thistle-milk and slug-slime, and rubbing off upon her naked arms sticky blights which, though snow-white on the apple-tree trunks, made madder stains on her skin; thus she drew quite near to Clare, still unobserved of him.

Tess was conscious of neither time nor space. The exaltation which she had described as being producible at will by gazing at a star, came now without any determination of hers; she undulated upon the thin notes of the second-hand harp, and their harmonies passed like breezes through her, bringing tears into her eyes. The floating pollen

seemed to be his notes made visible, and the dampness of the garden
the weeping of the garden's sensibility. Though near nightfall, the rank-
smelling weed-flowers glowed as if they would not close for intentness,
and the waves of colour mixed with the waves of sound. [Pp. 157-58] [7]

The romanticism in the simile of the pollen and the pathetic fallacy in
the simile of the damp garden of the last paragraph indicate that the
allusions are meant to project Tess's state of mind. She identifies in-
timately with her sensuous knowledge, and she genuinely "becomes"
the totality of her experiences of sense. More than any passage in the
novel, indeed, more than any passage in Hardy's fiction that I can
recall, here is a fully articulated evocation of a sensitivity too extreme
to survive the shocks of a powerful order of material Nature and the
grossness of the social world. And, thus, the entire basis for tragedy is
condensed into, and expressed through, this one paragraph and its
context.

The third paragraph of this description is deeply interesting.
One might first think its delicate, suggestive poetry an excrescence in
the midst of an otherwise obvious, and perhaps even awkward, effort
to render a mystical abandonment of self. Yet, contrary to most
readers' reaction that in this paragraph Tess is opposed to Nature, it
seems to me incontrovertible that the intention is to show Tess at
home in the garden. The smells do not seem to offend her, and she
moves through the garden familiarly, like a cat. Moreover, the associations of the garden's contents are not hostile to Tess, as has been
argued,[8] but congenial, as suggested by the beauty of the weeds, even
allowing for their offensive smells. Nor is Tess prefigured as a victim
in the third paragraph, for the verbs in the last sentence reveal that
she plays an active, not passive, part. In all, the "message," expressed
in David Lodge's words, is "that the force of this connection between
Tess and the natural world is to suggest the 'mad' passionate, non-
ethical quality of her sensibility."[9] Thus, in relation to my analysis
of the mystical quality of the fourth paragraph, the third paragraph
helps to underscore the non-moral and corresponsive nature of the
mystical experience.

Another such full mystical experience does not occur in *Tess of
the d'Urbervilles*, but there are other scenes which give the same
impression of Tess's unusual sensitivity to experience. Dressing for

her marriage to Angel, Tess "moved about in a mental cloud of many-coloured idealities, which eclipsed all sinister contingencies by its brightness" (p. 270). Going to church, "she knew that Angel was close to her; all the rest was a luminous mist. She was a sort of celestial person, who owed her being to poetry" (p. 271). As in the harp-playing episode, Tess's self-elevation on her wedding day suggests an ability to create her own intensity, to cut herself off from a world founded on rational relationships. Although a weakness and a cause for her destruction, this ability also accounts for her tragic power in the novel. She affirms the will to live and the will to enjoy in the face of what would be social disgrace if her past were to become known, and she makes this affirmation in response to an inner dynamism that triumphs over her awareness that conventional society considers her sexual guilt irredeemable.

The extensive reference to dreams and concern with the distinction between appearance and reality in *Tess of the d'Urbervilles* help to form a context for the underlying concept of mysticism. Dreams almost always involve disorientation from reality although, like Angel's sleepwalking "burial" of Tess, the most famous dream in the novel, they also lay bare inner realities and agonies of the dreamers. When Tess first visits Trantridge, Alec takes her on a tour of the estate, Tess obeying "like one in a dream" (p. 47). Angel dreams that Tess was of the lower class (p. 332; this, of course, is not a dream in the usual sense as much as it is a fancy). He almost talks to his hallucination of her while at his parents' house, her "cooing voice" disturbing the darkness (p. 337).

Dreamlike states also present psychological distortions, encouraging interpretations by the characters involved which are peculiar to them. Some of these states are developed through the surroundings. In the case of the dreamlike atmosphere attending the death of the horse Prince, the drowsiness of the participants makes them more receptive to hallucinatory suggestions: "Abraham, as he more fully awoke (for he had moved in a sort of trance so far), began to talk of the strange shapes assumed by the various dark objects against the sky; of this tree that looked like a raging tiger springing from a lair; of that which resembled a giant's head" (p. 32). Tess imagines that the trees and hedges they are passing are "attached to fantastic scenes outside reality." Examining her own life and thinking of her family's newly discovered "knightly ancestry," she comes closer to an actual sleeping dream, and falls asleep (pp. 34-35) before Prince is speared by the tongue of the speeding mail cart. Horrified by the violence of her awakening, Tess rushes to the front of Prince and is spattered with his blood, being marked, through Hardy's crude but effective symbolism, as one who will find pain and violent death on her own dark road of life. Another effective dreamlike scene is the entire sequence that leads to the seduction of Tess. The dance in Chaseborough takes place in a cloud of dust that from a distance combines obscurity and "a mist of yellow radiance," and that disguises the dancers in their "indistinctness" as "satyrs clasping nymphs — a multiplicity of Pans whirling a multiplicity of Syrinxes; Lotis attempting to elude Priapus, and always failing" ( p. 77). Once dancers finally find satisfactory partners, "the ecstasy and the dream began, in which emotion was the matter of the universe" (p. 79). The journey homeward is undertaken in an alcoholic stupor by most, leading to the argument between Car Darch and Tess. From this argument and the general uproar Tess flees with Alec on an "impulse" (p. 84). When Tess and Alec become lost, and the sense of darkness grows more dominant, Alec with the assistance of Tess's weariness, of her gratitude for his giving her father another horse (a gift he has just told her of), of her slumbering passionate nature, and presumably of a combination of surprise and force when he returns from a search for their road and finds her asleep, commits the crucial act in Tess's young life. It is the emphasis upon suggestibility, upon the tendency of minds to create a world amenable to their special situations that is pertinent in this lengthy dream-state preparation for the seduction.

Other scenes also convey a dreamlike state with rich reverberations. The baptism of little Sorrow (pp. 117-20) takes place at an "hour when fancy stalks outside reason, and malignant possibilities stand rock-firm as facts"; Tess has "lurid presentments" of the Devil and of little Sorrow in hell. Her excitement is conveyed to the other Durbeyfield children, and Tess is "transfigured." She speaks "so brightly that it seemed as though her face might have shone in the gloom surrounding her." The children look at her with reverence as she performs the baptism, as if they were looking at "a being large, towering, and awful — a divine personage with whom they had nothing in common." The entire scene is charged with urgency, with impal-

pable fear, that is alleviated with the coming of daylight. This lurid-
ness and urgency are not directly connected with the events. Hardy's
implication is that whether Sorrow is baptized matters only to Tess,
not to the fate of his soul. But Hardy's stress upon the connotativeness
of the baptism contributes importantly to the idea that Tess's sensitivity can achieve unusual heights.

All of Tess's wanderings and agony after Angel leaves to go to
Brazil partake of the quality of dream persecution, of the same evocative quality as the experiences of Dostoevski's and Kafka's heroes.
even if not as arcanely imaged. No part of her life in this section of the
novel adds more to this atmosphere than the scenes following Alec's
rediscovery of her. The threshing scene, especially as Tess becomes
progressively more harried by Alec's persistence during it, combines
lurid imagery of the machine and the mysteriousness of the man oper-
ating the steam engine to enforce a nightmarish conception of the
anarchy of consciousness:

> A little way off [from the threshing machine] was another *indistinct*
> figure; this one black, with a sustained hiss that spoke of strength very
> much in reserve. The long chimney running up beside an ash-tree, and
> the warmth which radiated from the spot, explained without the neces-
> sity of much daylight that here was the engine which was to act as the
> *primum mobile* of this little world. By the engine stood a dark motion-
> less being, a sooty and grimy embodiment of tallness, *in a sort of trance,*
> with a heap of coals by his side: it was the engine-man. The isolation
> of his manner and colour lent him the appearance of a creature from
> Tophet, who had strayed into the pellucid smokelessness of this region
> of yellow grain and pale soil, with which he had nothing in common,
> *to amaze and to discompose* its aborigines.
>
> *What he looked he felt.* He was in the agricultural world, but not
> of it. He served fire and smoke; these denizens of the fields served
> vegetation, weather, frost, and sun. He travelled with his engine 'from
> farm to farm, from county to county, for as yet the steam threshing-
> machine was itinerant in this part of Wessex. He spoke in a strange
> northern accent; *his thoughts being turned inwards upon himself,* his
> eye on his iron charge, *hardly perceiving the scenes around him,* and
> caring for them not at all: holding only strictly necessary intercourse
> with the natives, as if some ancient doom compelled him to wander
> here against his will in the service of his Plutonic master. The long strap
> which ran from the driving-wheel of his engine to the red thresher under
> the rick was the sole tie-line between agriculture and him. [Pp. 414-15;
> my italics]

The engine man is seen scarcely at all in his concrete reality. Through simultaneous perspectives upon his appearance and his role he is made to exist as an image of indefinable threat. His consciousness dislocates him from the material rural life around him; he is nearly co-identical with the machine that is at once his "charge" and his "master"; and his aloof and scornful demeanor emphasizes his potential destructiveness to a world in which he refuses to participate imaginatively. This section of the story is climaxed by Tess's striking Alec while they are on the rick and then patiently waiting to be beaten: "Once victim, always victim — that's the law!" (p. 423). Hardy presses home the tension raised in Tess by Alec's renewed persecution. Alec leaves her on the haystack, after reminding her that "I was your master once! I will be your master again. If you are any man's wife you are mine!" Stunned and speechless, Tess resumes her work "as one in a dream" (p. 423). Amplifying the sense of dream persecution is the subsequent garden scene, in which Alec appears to Tess in the midst of smoldering fires and smoke like a pursuing devil (a description that underscores his resemblance to the threshing-machine engine-man as a threatening outlander), ominously preceding by minutes the death of Tess's father (pp. 443-46). Since the Durbeyfield house was a lifehold and Tess's father was the third and last life for which the house was leased, Tess's family is made homeless, opening Tess to new — and irresistible — blandishments by Alec.

Another carefully developed dream scene is the meeting between Tess and Angel in the front room of the Bournemouth rooming house where Tess is living with Alec in return for his support of her family. Tess seems to feel "like a fugitive in a dream, who tries to move away, but cannot" (pp. 483-84). Both seem to want "something to shelter them from reality"; they are unable to express themselves either silently or with speech. A total barrier is set up between them: Angel, it seems, goes into a catatonic trance, for he "finds" after a few moments that Tess has left the room; and a minute or two later he "finds" himself in the street, "walking along he did not know whither." The presentation of this meeting, of course, indicates more clearly than authorial explicitness could that the consciousnesses of the two undergo horror and shock before they become adjusted to the new situation. This scene presents the final turn of the screw to Tess's dilemma, for in an indirect and ironic way the sensitivity of Tess and

Angel at their meeting is responsible for her tragic act in killing Alec. Angel has presumably achieved psychic growth in Brazil, has come to recognize that he should judge Tess by her inclination, not her acts. And he vaguely realizes, in a manner consistent with the novel's stress upon the importance of subjectivity of consciousness, "that his original Tess had spiritually ceased to recognize the body before him as hers—allowing it to drift, like a corpse upon the current, in a direction dissociated from its living will." Tess says to him, "These clothes are what he's put upon me: I didn't care what he did wi' me!" But when he sees her fresh from the bed of the man he had thought was entirely in her past, he cannot adjust rapidly to the situation, although "Ah—it is my fault!" indicates that in time he can recover from even this shock.[10] Ironically, instead of struggling to understand immediately, he cannot escape the dreamlike state: he "unconsciously" eats breakfast and waits numbly for a train to take him from Bournemouth. Although Angel cannot rationally be blamed for Alec's death, Alec dies because Angel—like Conrad's Lord Jim—is unable to act in an unanticipated situation.

The motif of appearance-reality substantiates the genuineness of the mysticism in the novel. It reveals the shallowness of some characters' pretension to profound experience and dignifies the intensity of experiences that are not called into question. Moreover, it stresses the possibility of mystical experience as an underlying basis of the novel. Some of the more striking instances of this motif are about alcoholic events, when there is a kind of false mysticism: the drinker in a stupor thinks he is of special importance. For instance, Mrs. Durbeyfield delights in going to Rolliver's tavern with her husband. "A sort of halo, an occidental glow, came over life then. Troubles and other realities took on themselves a metaphysical impalpability, sinking to mere mental phenomena for serene contemplation, and no longer stood as pressing concretions which chafed body and soul" (p. 23). Again, the descriptions of the drunken field-folk perceiving themselves akin to nature suggest the grandeur one places upon himself falsely (as compared to Tess's honest hopes of revivifying her life in going to Talbothays):

> Yet however terrestrial and lumpy their appearance just now to the
> mean unglamoured eye, to themselves the case was different. They

followed the road with a sensation that they were soaring along in a supporting medium, possessed of original and profound thoughts, themselves and surrounding nature forming an organism of which all the parts harmoniously and joyously interpenetrated each other. They were as sublime as the moon and stars above them, and the moon and stars were as ardent as they. [Pp. 80-81]

Like Joan Durbeyfield in the pub, each drunken peasant has a halo invisible to everyone else (caused by the moon) and feels himself in harmony with Nature (p. 84).

Angel, too, experiences much the same delusion, although with him it is self-imposed rather than inspired by alcohol. He walks with Tess during their courtship in the "spectral, half-compounded, aqueous light which pervaded the open mead," and etherealizes and allegorizes Tess — inaccurately, and to Tess's displeasure:

She looked ghostly, as if she were merely a soul at large. In reality her face, without appearing to do so, had caught the cold gleam of day from the north-east; his own face, though he did not think of it, wore the same aspect to her.

It was then, as has been said, that she impressed him most deeply. She was no longer the milkmaid, but a visionary essence of woman — a whole sex condensed into one typical form. He called her Artemis, Demeter, and other fanciful names half teasingly, which she did not like because she did not understand them.

"Call me Tess," she would say askance; and he did.

Then it would grow lighter, and her features would become simply feminine; they had changed from those of a divinity who could confer bliss to those of a being who craved it. [Pp. 167-68][11]

What may serve as an authorial annotation to this passage is a later description of the difference between Angel's infatuation and the reality of Tess: "How very lovable her face was to him. Yet there was nothing ethereal about it; all was real vitality, real warmth, real incarnation" (p. 192). Angel's romantic consciousness is a dangerous element in the novel. During the early morning time of the "luminous gloom," Angel thinks of the "Resurrection hour." Ironically, he does not think that the woman at his side might be the Magdalen (p. 167). A double irony is that even if he knew Tess to be Madgalen, he is not capable of accepting her spiritual or psychological purity; this is made clear when Tess confesses her past, and Angel cannot cope with the truth of her situation. "He argued erroneously when he said to himself that her heart was not indexed in the honest freshness of her face; but Tess had no advocate to set him right" (p. 301). On the day following her confession, he is equally incapable of seeing her aright: "She looked absolutely pure. Nature, in her fantastic trickery, had set such a seal of maidenhood upon Tess's countenance that he gazed at her with a stupefied air" (pp. 303-304). Even Tess can be deluded by appearances. She overestimates Angel (p. 246) and thinks that Angel's parents will despise her as a mendicant if she asks for help after Angel leaves her (p. 349). In a more important sequence, she accepts the arrogant complacency of Angel's brothers as evidence that Mr. Clare would be as cold and distant as his sons (p. 384). These examples of misguided consciousness suggest the ambiguity at the heart of the mental construct for tragedy that Hardy has organized. Not only is each individual isolated within himself; he is not always accurate in his perspective.


## II


All the techniques which Hardy uses to emphasize the supremacy of individual feeling are closely related. For example, the relativity of perspective, which isolates everyone's opinion and feeling, makes the value of these feelings dependent on the individual's particular, temporary stance. In *Tess of the d'Urbervilles*, each judgment is tentative, usually made by only one character, presented in such a way as to make it impossible for the reader to commit himself fully to that viewpoint. I have noted that *reality* is only infrequently defined by Hardy. In other words, Hardy customarily forces the reader back to the individual consciousness; he makes tragedy reside in the single consciousness that we see reacting to the particular situation.

Perhaps the clearest account Hardy gives of the necessity to note the perspective from which an opinion stems is his ironic description of the death of Sorrow:

So passed away Sorrow the Undesired — that intrusive creature, that

bastard gift of shameless Nature who respects not the social law; a waif
to whom eternal Time had been a matter of days merely, who knew not
that such things as years and centuries ever were; to whom the cottage
interior was the universe, the week's weather climate, new-born baby-
hood human existence, and the instinct to suck human knowledge.
[Pp. 120-21]

The relationship between this paragraph and that quoted earlier in
which Hardy defends "subjective experiences" as the basis for measuring the magnitude of lives (p. 198) is obvious. In each, the only perspective that matters is that of the particular individual. Similar to
these passages is one implying Tess's aggrandizement of the humble
marmalade jar that holds flowers on Sorrow's grave. "What matter
was it that on the outside of the jar the eye of mere observation noted
the words 'Keelwell's Marmalade'? The eye of maternal affection did
not see them in its vision of higher things" (p. 123).

It is necessary, of course, that the perceiver be in a suitable
position and state of mind to see "truth." For example, before Angel
had come to Talbothays, he had anticipated associating with rural
Hodges who were personified by the newspapers as pitiable dummies,
but he finds that rural people are as individualistic and their lives as
unmonotonous as those of people in higher social levels (pp. 151-53,
216).

Angel takes as many relativist positions as anyone in the novel.
Indeed, his attitudes toward ancient families are one of the keys to
an interpretation of the novel as subjective. Although initially undogmatic about the matter, he says that while he is politically skeptical of
the value of old families, he is attached to them "lyrically, dramatically, and even historically" (p. 213). When he discovers, in the midst
of his infatuation with Tess, that she is a d'Urberville, he admits that
he hates the "aristocratic principle of blood" and discounts all pedi-
grees but spiritual ones. But he calmly ignores his own animus and
says he is "extremely interested" in Tess's ancestry, although he never
explains why he is interested or why his interest is superior to his
principled dislike (pp. 241-42). When he feels Tess's parentage might
be a welcome possession to impress his parents with, he unduly prizes
her blood lines: "Perhaps Tess's lineage had more value for himself
than for anybody in the world besides" (p. 268). Angel's bafflement
at learning of Tess's affair with Alec has him returning, with a ven-

geance, to his earlier unfavorable view of the aristocracy: "I cannot help associating your decline as a family with this other fact — of your want of firmness. Decrepit families imply decrepit wills, decrepit conduct. Heaven, why did you give me a handle for despising you more by informing me of your descent! Here was I thinking you a new-sprung child of nature; there were you, the belated seedling of an effete aristocracy!" (p. 297). Angel convinces himself that all of his unhappiness has been caused by Tess's being a d'Urberville; he criticizes himself for not "stoically" abandoning her "in fidelity to his principles" when he learned that she "came of that exhausted ancient line" (p. 332). Finally, after the stranger in Brazil encourages Angel to believe in Tess's essential purity of motive, Angel again shifts his position concerning the d'Urberville family. "The historic interest of her family...touched his sentiments now. Why had he not known the difference between the political value and the imaginative value of these things?" (p. 436). He had, of course, once known this difference, as the passage quoted above attests (p. 213). This lack of self-knowledge implies that Angel's growth in Brazil is not complete; he is nearly as fanciful now as before, with primarily the milder view of Tess to mark a stage of personal growth.

Angel himself recognizes the relativity of his position and his situation in being married to Tess, following her revelation of her affair with Alec. He scorns her idea of suicide: "It is nonsense to have such thoughts in this kind of case, which is rather one for satirical laughter than for tragedy. You don't in the least understand the quality of the mishap. It would be viewed in the light of a joke by nine-tenths of the world if it were known" (pp. 298-99). In time Angel comes to see the relative importance of Tess to the larger world, and to nature itself. In tracing Tess's journey back to Marlott, he talks to the new residents of the Durbeyfield cottage:

> The new residents . . . |took| as much interest in their own doings as if the homestead had never passed its primal time in conjunction with the histories of others, beside which the histories of these were but as a tale told by an idiot. They walked about the garden paths with thoughts of their own concerns entirely uppermost, bringing their actions at every moment into jarring collision with the dim ghosts behind them, talking as though the time when Tess lived there were not one whit intenser in story than now. Even the spring birds sang over

their heads as if they thought there was nobody missing in particular.
[Pp. 476-77]

Angel's new perspective upon life is to a large degree influenced by the remarks made by the stranger in Brazil, who had traveled widely. "To his cosmopolitan mind such deviations [as Tess's] from the social norm, so immense to domesticity, were no more than are the irregularities of vale and mountain-chain to the whole terrestrial curve. He viewed the matter in quite a different light from Angel" (p. 434). These views, which explicitly lower Tess's external stature and the significance of her acts as "sins," clearly locate the tragic element of the novel in the consciousnesses of the characters.

Tess too looks at particular things from particular stances, a mode of perception which limits the validity of any one insight. When she and Angel return briefly to Talbothays after their wedding trip and her wedding-night confessions, she views the landscape of Talbothays in a different light from when they had been courting there. "The gold of the summer picture was now gray, the colours mean, the rich soil mud, and the river cold" (p. 321). Of course, the season is winter, not summer; but it had been winter on their wedding day, too. Hardy does not describe the setting until it reflects their state of mind (see pp. 270-72).

The novel's basis in subjectivity and in relativity of truth calls attention to point of view. Several quotations given above clearly present opinions or interpretations of situations as determined by the perceiver. In a strictly technical sense, the point of view or narrative perspective in *Tess of the d'Urbervilles* is omniscient. But in a practical or aesthetic sense, Hardy maneuvers his point of view in order to communicate not the absolute truth of a situation but the innumerable ways of looking at a situation.[12]

The lack of a moral imperative creates an atmosphere in which every man has his own truth, and has it, moreover, in only a limited way. In passages involving the appearance-reality motif, for instance, Hardy frequently observes that what a character feels is not accurate. He remarks that Tess's and Angel's physical closeness during their brief return to the dairy would have appeared to be peculiarly pitiable "to one who should have seen it truly" (p. 322). Again, Tess's belief that human nature is different in Blackmoor Vale and Flintcomb-Ash is refuted parenthetically by the narrator (p. 431). Hardy, with his ironist's pencil busily annotating the metaphysics of nature's seeming concern for Tess's life, occasionally reminds the reader that man attributes to nature a sense of his self that in fact is not shared by nature. As Tess descends to the Valley of the Dairies, reinvigorated with life partly inspired by the fecundity of the scene and atmosphere, "she felt akin to the landscape" (p. 132). But Hardy observes that she was "of no more consequence to the surroundings than... a fly on a billiard-table." A humdrum rural image reinforces the reality of Tess's isolation. The barking of a dog "was not the expression of the valley's consciousness that beautiful Tess had arrived, but the ordinary announcement of milking-time — half-past four o'clock, when the dairymen set about getting in the cows" (p. 136).

At times it is difficult to separate the position of the omniscient storyteller (or *persona*) from that of one of the characters. On Angel's wedding night, there is a shifting between Angel and the *persona*. After Tess confesses her past to Angel, there is a combination of Angel's agonized horror and the narrator's detached analysis. "The complexion even of external things seemed to suffer transmutation. ...The fire in the grate looked impish — demoniacally funny, as if it did not care in the least about her strait. The fender grinned idly, as if it too did not care. The light from the water-bottle was merely engaged in a chromatic problem. All material objects around announced their irresponsibility with terrible iteration. And yet nothing had changed since the moments when he had been kissing her; or rather, nothing in the substance of things. But the essence of things had changed" (p. 291). Shortly, Angel's perspective on the things around him is shown to be distorted by his sense of having been cheated: "Sinister design lurked in the woman's features [a painting of a d'Urberville woman], a concentrated purpose of revenge on the other sex — so it seemed to him then" (p. 300). This is obviously Angel's viewpoint, modified by the *persona's* detachment. A description of Angel's "small compressed mouth" and the "terribly sterile expression" on his face during this scene is obviously the *persona* speaking. But the final paragraph is of indeterminate origin, leaving undecided the significance of Angel's agony: "He reclined on his couch in the sitting-room, and extinguished the light. The night came in, and took up its place there, unconcerned and indifferent; the night which had already swallowed up his happiness, and was now digesting it listlessly; and was ready to swallow up the happiness of a thousand other people with as little disturbance or change of mien" (p. 301). While in method this seems to be the omniscient narrator, the despairing tone in which man's inconsequence is announced is clearly contradictory to the idea of calm forebearance which Angel comes in contact with in Brazil, the idea that man can make his happiness in spite of nature's indifference. Moreover, the indifference of nature in the Brazil sections encourages tolerance on the level of human relationships; here during the end of the wedding-night scene, nature's attitude is inseparable from Angel's bleak mien. The weight of these considerations supports the idea that this paragraph represents Angel's subjective viewpoint, but the evidence is not conclusive.

The point of view at times amplifies directly the emphasis upon subjectivity. Indeed, the passage quoted above concerning the magnitude of subjective experiences is given from Angel's point of view; and the subsequent paragraph in the novel communicates both Angel's fastidiousness and the somewhat pompous evaluation he makes of his own life:

> This consciousness upon which he had intruded was the single opportunity of existence ever vouchsafed to Tess by an unsympathetic First Cause — her all; her every and only chance. How then should he look upon her as of less consequence than himself; as a pretty trifle to caress and grow weary of; and not deal in the greatest seriousness with the affection which he knew that he had awakened in her — so fervid and so impressionable as she was under her reserve; in order that it might not agonize and wreck her? [P. 199]

The subjectivity of *Tess of the d'Urbervilles* is also enhanced through Hardy's characteristic method of attributing lifelike qualities to inanimate objects. This animism is particularly obvious in scenes concerning Tess herself. The field on Flintcomb-Ash in which Tess works is portrayed as a human face. "It was a complexion without features, as if a face, from chin to brow, should be only an expanse of skin. The sky wore, in another colour, the same likeness; a white vacuity of countenance with the lineaments gone" (pp. 363-64). The threshing machine that Tess works on at Flintcomb-Ash is a "red tyrant that the women had come to serve . . . [which] kept up a despotic demand upon the endurance of their muscles and nerves" (p. 414); and the straw produced by the machine is alluded to as the *"faeces* of the same buzzing red glutton" (p. 424). These uses of animism are significant primarily because they connect Tess with the source of naturalistic power in her universe; we have already noted that she leaves her parents' home in Marlott when "the stir of generation . . . moved her, as it moved the wild animals, and made her passionate to go" (p. 126). Even though Tess misunderstands the degree to which there is an affinity between nature's purpose and mankind's, Hardy points out frequently that there is an inescapable bond between the human and the natural scene: "Some spirit within her rose automatically as the sap in the twigs. It [brought] . . . the invincible instinct towards self-delight," the same instinct that later is called "the inherent will to enjoy" and is contrasted with "the circumstantial will against enjoyment" (p. 365). Tess, the conscious individual, becomes confronted with the great natural forces which express themselves through her. It is possible to read this situation as prohibiting tragedy because of its implication of the impossibility of free choice. To be sure, numerous scenes and passages link the psychological state of the individual to the scene or landscape in which he finds himself, such as Tess's willing absorption into the lush fertility of the Valley of the Froom and her dejected endurance and blighted spirit at Flintcomb-Ash. The customary reading of these passages has seen Hardy paralleling Tess's state of mind with her environment in order to heighten the reader's identification with the action and to reduce Tess to a "figment with feelings." Generally critics have taken this parallelism as an amplification of man's identification with Nature and thus of his essential will-lessness or his inability to strike a free pose;[13] but such readings overlook Tess's active choices and her moments of resistance to natural impulse which make her a responsible sufferer. Moreover, several theorists of tragedy suggest that this correspondence between forces impelling the actor/sufferer and primary qualities of the universe helps to account for the claustrophobic relevance of every detail in tragic art.[14]

    In any case, the emphasis throughout the novel upon the subjective creation of significance in a sensitive and serious consciousness is the more important indication of the origin of the tragic response aroused by Hardy. However insignificant in an absolute sense the individual might be, in his own subjective existence he is of consummate importance. The destruction of the individual might indeed be microcosmic and symbolic; the novel contains adequate evidence for such a view. But more important in *Tess of the d'Urbervilles* than the symbolic value of the fatedness of the individual is the self-status of the individual. Entirely within himself he constitutes a world of moral vigor.[15] A particular moral stance may be good only for the fleeting moment in which it is taken, but then the ongoing moment here is the only meaningful unit of time in relation to morality. The physical world has substantial dimensions and a variety of more or less permanent forms; but the temporal conditions of human life are immediateness and instability. As Hardy makes clear in referring to the indifference of the new inhabitants of the Durbeyfield home toward the most intense feelings and activities of the old inhabitants, the capability of creating tragedy resides only in the character who feels the tragedy. In the novel, the situations of the characters also allow the reader to feel tragedy precisely because Hardy in his portrayal of Tess creates within the reader an awareness of the extent of her psychic sufferings. Through the enhancement of the subjectivity by means of the tactics I have described, Hardy not only allows but also requires the reader to create for himself his individual view of Tess, her essential personality. There are no absolutes in Tess's personality: she is both pure and corrupted, she is both idealistic and sensual; and no one in the novel understands her. Because Hardy breaks down all dispositions toward Tess, she is made capable of sustaining, in irresolvable contradiction and ambiguity, the awareness of her that the individual reader gains through the interreaction of his consciousness with hers and with those of the people around her. The attraction of *Tess of the d'Urbervilles* as a tragedy is this absorptive feature, which permits the reader to participate in tragic vision on his own terms. Every aspect of the novel's form glides away from a prescribed significance; nothing human "means" outside itself. The psychic state of subjectivity, at once aesthetic and moral, defines the nature of the tragedy that *Tess of the d'Urbervilles* fulfills.

# 7

## JUDE THE OBSCURE:

*Doctrine or Distanced Narrator?*

In *The Woodlanders* and *Tess of the d'Urbervilles* Hardy establishes universal potentiality for tragedy by different methods, employing forms that are increasingly less mechanical in their influence upon the presentation of the narrative. *Jude the Obscure* continues this development and traces, like *Tess of the d'Urbervilles,* the protagonist's movement through a number of reactions to dilemmas. But the final adequacy of the protagonist's individual judgments and the true nature of the experiences that mark his course are more of an issue in this novel than they are in *Tess.* Jude's perceptions are more directly and more frequently called into question through a confluence of judgments and of evaluations of the experiences.

The democratization of tragedy implied in *The Woodlanders* and *Tess of the d'Urbervilles* is both enhanced and modified in *Jude the Obscure*. It is enhanced by the suggestion that each of the differing standards of judgment has merit; it is modified insofar as external evaluations of the protagonist's impressions about the conditions of life weaken the self-validation of tragic consciousness, which is at the core of the method of *Tess of the d'Urbervilles.* Though mysticism is not part of Jude's makeup, the power of this novel still comes from the intensity of mental experience. But greater attention is given in *Jude the Obscure* than in *Tess of the d'Urbervilles* whether

it is necessary that the protagonist experience as much suffering as he
or she does.

The process of evaluation that takes place is of central importance in discerning the quality of the novel, for the customary reaction
to *Jude the Obscure* is that while an evaluation may be taking place,
it is an evaluation by the storyteller himself, speaking *in propria
persona*. Readers with this reaction to the novel believe that Hardy
has lost control of his art — that, beset by a mounting conviction that
society is badly organized for humane existence and by the final dis-
integration of his own marital peace, he has seized upon his story idea
of blighted intellectual and emotional aspiration to vent his own feelings of frustration and bitterness.

It is a common observation in Hardy criticism that his last novels,
especially *Jude the Obscure*, evince increasingly personal and
aesthetically undisciplined meditations on human fate and attacks on
certain social institutions.[1] Morton Dauwen Zabel puts the matter
directly: *Jude the Obscure* "was written out of a deliberate and summary intention. It was meant to bring Hardy's reading of the human
fate to its most complete and exhaustive statement."[2] For Carl Weber,
the novel is simply unconstrained propaganda: "If Hardy failed, as he
did, it was not because the novel, as an art-form, is unfitted to bring
about social reform; it was because Hardy's aim was too sweeping,
his skill too defective, and — it must be admitted — his artistic control too frenzied."[3] Barbara Hardy analyzes *Jude the Obscure* as
representative of dogmatic form in fiction. She sees it in relation to
novels in which Providence is illustrated, such as *Robinson Crusoe*
and *Jane Eyre,* although *Jude the Obscure,* unlike them, is a novel in
which Providence always works against characters' happiness rather
than for it.[4] Barbara Hardy puts the case well; but in strange contrast to the richness of her insight into Defoe's and Brontë's novels,
she makes no effort to relate the power of *Jude the Obscure* (which
she concedes) to the idea of dogmatic improvidence (of which she
disapproves).

A spokesman for those who think that Hardy's personal involvement in the novel prevents its achieving tragedy is Arthur Mizener.[5]
Although he says that the novel is not autobiographical "in the
specific sense," Mizener believes that Hardy identifies so closely with
the protagonist and with the novel's dilemmas that the author's doc-

trines become the only test of values. In arguing that there is no source "outside of time" for the idealism that in *Jude the Obscure* measures the world and finds it wanting, Mizener establishes the source within Hardy's meliorism, which posits a particular, realizable paradise on earth. "There is no basic, unresolvable tragic tension between the real and the ideal in [Hardy's] attitude, and there is as a consequence no tragic tension in the formal structure it invokes as its representation."[6]

None of these judgments is persuasive. We have already seen Hardy's growing competence in developing methods of organization and presentation that best advance his concept of a story and its significance; and it is illogical to accept without close scrutiny the idea that at the apex of his creativity and craftsmanship in prose he became a proselytizer at the expense of his art. This is not to suggest that he is a cold or impersonal novelist. Far from that, he is deeply implicated in all of his great novels, and judgments on life and characters abound. Indeed, his appeal is largely in his readers' awareness that they are not being asked to sympathize with characters toward whom the author is indifferent. But authorial implication or even commitment does not preclude controlled presentation. An increasing subtlety in the handling of one aspect of narrative art has its culmination in *Jude the Obscure*; acknowledgment of this aspect of narration gives us a new view into the nature of the supposed didacticism of Hardy's later novels and permits us to understand how the novel achieves the objectivity and balance of tragedy.

This aspect of narration is authorial distance, the establishing of a situation in which the author cannot be identified with his characters, nor his ideas with theirs. In fact, the ideas of the author and of his characters may be identical or at least closely similar, which is usually considered the situation in Hardy's fiction;[7] but in the individual piece of fiction itself, this co-identity is disguised or obscured. Hardy remarks in *Jude the Obscure*: "The purpose of a chronicler of moods and deeds does not require him to express his personal views upon the grave controversy above given [Jude and Sue's decision not to marry]" (p. 348). Authorial distance creates the impression that characters have a life of their own in the sense that the author is in some way detached from both the machinations which his characters undergo at his hands and the concerns which his characters feel. With authorial distance, the ostensibly omniscient narrator stands in one of three possible relationships to his story: the objective and entirely removed storyteller (Flaubert for long stretches in *Madame Bovary*); the *persona* whose dominant mind-set is established by his style of presentation, and whose status is essentially that of another character (Thackeray in *Vanity Fair*); or a superior mentality evaluating the actions being described (Eliot in *Middlemarch*). There are, of course, any number of variations upon these three stances, just as there are numerous variations upon the principle of authorial distance. Both Trollope and Meredith, while given to philosophizing and interjecting advice to the reader on how to react to their fictions, are essentially *personas* who do not alter the progress of the fictional action, which has its own logic. Dickens, on the other hand, creates a measure of distance by the flamboyance of syntax and rhetoric and by the fantastic quality of a part of his fictions, but his self-involvement is never in doubt, his loyalties never ambiguous (except in the unfinished *Mystery of Edwin Drood*).

The genesis of *Jude the Obscure*, as evidenced by Hardy's famous remark in a letter to Edmund Gosse, lends credence to my suggestion concerning his conscious artistry: "Your review (of *Jude the Obscure*) is the most discriminating that has yet appeared. It required an artist to see that the plot is almost geometrically constructed —I ought not to say *constructed*, for, beyond a certain point, the characters necessitated it, and I simply let it come" (*Later Years*, p. 40). Hardy's emphasis upon the precise construction of the novel suggests his awareness of the artistry; his emphasis upon the self-direction of the characters' actions suggests that he was not, at least consciously or admittedly, forcing the entities of his fiction to illustrate a preconceived set of principles. Without using the critical term *authorial distance*, Hardy clearly distinguishes between himself and his characters. His statement that he "simply let it come" does not mean that he was an automatic writer, of course, but that the plot develops from the interactions of the characters. However unplanned may be the characters' actions, the presentation (and thereby the significance) is always Hardy's.

# I

The most effective technique to promote the sense of authorial distance in *Jude the Obscure* is manipulation of point of view. Although Hardy's use of point of view has been noted in a number of contexts in this study, in *Jude the Obscure* the degree of artistic accomplishment depends more upon this technique than in his other novels. It might be well, however, to look first at other methods which help to establish a framework of action and expectation that is congenial for his use of point of view. A central technique for the creation of distance in all of his novels is abruptness, both of action and of scene change — a technique often described as *grotesque, expressionistic,* and *symbolic distortion*; therefore, any attempt to enumerate exhaustively the abrupt actions and scenes in *Jude the Obscure* is unnecessary. Similarly, the brevity and even absence of explanations of character motivation complement the abruptness of action. Hardy ordinarily does not refine the characterizations of his actors. His grandiose efforts to evoke heroic dimensions to Clym and Eustacia in his early presentations of them are notable exceptions to his usual practice, and despite the pyrotechnic references to gods and heroes and solemnities of symbolic action, the evocations are not entirely successful.

Hardy's novels usually begin fast; a customary feature is the "given" quality of much of the situation. Examples are the cinematographic zeroing-in on Henchard and Susan walking along a dusty road, with no motivation specified for their emotional estrangement; and the impulsive disclosure of genealogical information by Parson Tringham to Tess's father. The rapidity with which Hardy enters upon basic issues in *Jude the Obscure*, without authorial direction in such matters as atmosphere and character motivation, exceeds even his customary pace. By the third page Jude is portrayed as a meditative child "who has felt the pricks of life somewhat before his time"; and in the following chapter he identifies with his fellow-sufferers, the birds he has been employed to keep out of Farmer Troutham's fields (p. 11). He muses on his disgrace at being discharged by Troutham and on the possibility that he "might be a burden to his great-aunt for life" (p. 13), and he laments the horridness of "Nature's logic" (p. 15). The context of this last lamentation is helpful in getting at the effects of Hardy's technique. After his aunt has with relative sternness chastized Jude for demeaning her by giving unsatisfactory service to a farmer who had once been her father's journeyman, Jude goes outside to lie "on a heap of litter near the pig-sty" and to ruminate:

Growing up brought responsibilities, he found. Events did not rhyme quite as he had thought. Nature's logic was too horrid for him to care for. That mercy towards one set of creatures was cruelty towards another sickened his sense of harmony. As you got older, and felt yourself to be at the centre of your time, and not at a point in its circumference, as you had felt when you were little, you were seized with a sort of shuddering, he perceived. All around you there seemed to be something glaring, garish, rattling, and the noises and glares hit upon the little cell called your life, and shook it, and warped it. [P. 15]

Here we have Jude's analysis, not Hardy's. Although the views are familiar to us from other sources,[8] now Hardy is careful to dissociate himself from them in the novel. For our present purposes Jude's ruminations are notable because of their incompleteness. By this stage in the novel Hardy has not had time to justify aesthetically Jude's quality of mind, at once frenetic and profound. The reader has not yet learned of Jude's previous life; he can logically grasp only that his life with "Mrs. Fawley" is not entirely happy. The critical reader must infer, then, either that Hardy begins the book in a fury without thought of justifying his character's states of mind (if we assume that Hardy enters the novel in a close and personal way), or that he is attempting to impress upon the reader the individuality of Jude's views.[9] The very absence of any rationale for Jude's views makes them his own in a peculiarly individual manner. They characterize his outlook on life more pointedly because they are dissociated from any experience of Jude's observed by the reader. In a sense, Hardy permits the reader to anticipate the entire course of Jude's life by thus having Jude philosophize before making any effort to justify the implied tenets of the philosophy. After being presented with an experience-less protagonist with this state of mind in the opening scenes, only a very obtuse reader could plan to read about the triumph of the protagonist, because this sort of mind-set turns all triumph to gall and remorse.

To the extent that this view of life keenly marks the beholder, *Jude the Obscure* begins more abruptly and modernistically than *The Mayor of Casterbridge*, frequently proposed as the best illustration of Hardy's ability to begin a story without prefatory matter. Similar in quality to the beginning of *Jude the Obscure* is the beginning of *Tess of the d'Urbervilles,* in which a "chance" and uncharacteristic failure in discretion by Parson Tringham initiates a chain of events and statements that includes Tess's confession of belief to her brother that theirs is a blighted world. In both *Tess of the d'Urbervilles* and *Jude the Obscure,* the early declarations of disillusionment subsequently find more than adequate justification; but the contexts in which they appear indicate that they are meant to characterize the speakers and to establish the tone of the novel rather than to express the author's philosophy.

Another aspect of abruptness as a technique in Hardy's fiction is the conciseness of scene presentation and the rapidity of scene change. Events occur in quick succession, usually with motivation once the novel is under way, but seldom with the full motivation that the apparent significance of an act would seem to require. This rapidity and compression give to Hardy's fiction the quality of sensationalism that his theorizing on the art of fiction calls for: "A story must be exceptional enough to justify its telling. We tale-tellers are all Ancient Mariners, and none of us is warranted in stopping Wedding Guests (in other words, the hurrying public) unless he has something more unusual to relate than the ordinary experience of every average man and woman" (*Later Years*, pp. 15-16). The sensationalism is evident in all the novels. Hardy in hindsight thought it weakened *The Mayor of Casterbridge,* although most readers are likely to feel that the rapidity of plot complications strengthens the fabric of tragic inevitability in the clash between Henchard and Farfrae. In *Tess of the d'Urbervilles* and *Jude the Obscure,* sensationalism is intensified by change in geographic scene; indeed, it has been argued that adding a new, geographic dimension to sensationalism compensates for the loss of unity of place in Hardy's last two experiments in tragedy.[10] A typical sequence in *Jude the Obscure* — which consumes only five-and-a-half pages of narration — takes Jude on a visit from Christminster to Marygreen to visit his sick aunt, where he learns other fascinating details about Sue's tomboy youth that make him desire her the more and where he talks to his former neighbors about the glories of Christminster. Reminded thereby that he must soon take some practical steps to enter a college, Jude on the trip back to Christminster decides to obtain the advice of a don and selects five Heads of Houses to write to (pp. 130-35). This sequence gives the impression of the heedless plunging-ahead of human behavior and the close interrelatedness of actions. It effects authorial distance by emphasizing the distance between the author and the situation he has created. The characters are forced to exist according to whatever authority their words and actions grant them, because the author does not establish an existence for them through detailed motivation and analysis. Novels sometimes convey the impression that the characters are puppets, moved about and disposed of at the author's will with no concern for plausibility. Hardy was at one time accused of this sort of manipulation; then critics saw that his characters were not controlled by him as much as by the universe, that is, by the universe's principle of orderliness: causality. This insight is only a limited advance in critical logic, but it is a significant one, for it shatters the widely held theory that Hardy is a sort of archetype of the author as clumsy craftsman. The next step in critical logic is also limited, but again it is significant. That step is the impetus of this chapter: the narrator is separate from the tale he tells; in other words, the attacks on man's state in the universe, in this world, and in marriage come from the characters. I do not deny that Hardy may agree with his characters. Indeed, it is very likely that he agrees with them at various points, despite the explicit disclaimer about *Jude the Obscure* that he gives in *Later Years* (p. 41): "My own views [on marriage] are not expressed therein." But our knowledge of Hardy's opinions comes from biography, from his reputation built up by outraged reviewers who used personal invective to combat his supposedly revolutionary ideas, and from his letters to friends and contributions to symposia." If we had only the novel, we could be no more confident about Hardy's personal opinions than we are now of Henry James's opinions concerning the central moral issues of "The Pupil," "The Turn of the Screw," or "The Liar." And as with James, the reason we are unable to pin on Hardy the ideas in *Jude the Obscure* is the use he makes of point of view.

It should be emphasized, though, that Hardy's use of point of view is not the same as James's. In Hardy, the perspective upon the action is subordinate in importance to the action itself. With James, on the other hand, point of view is the most influential matter in the story. In "The Liar," for instance, interpretation of or reaction to the narrator necessarily precedes an interpretation of the relative morality of Lyon and Capadosa. The interpretation of *Jude the Obscure* undergoes a certain alteration of emphasis when Hardy's use of point of view in the novel is understood; but it requires less shift in attitude than becomes necessary for the reader who initially accepts Lyon's judgments simply because he is the narrator and then realizes the profound range of deceptiveness and baseness in Lyon himself.

## II

It is customary to take Hardy's narrative stance as that of the traditional omniscient narrator, who observes all that is worth knowing and who reveals his knowledge to the reader effusively, even though he is willing to hold back certain information for the sake of suspense. But Hardy is seldom this sort of loose-tongued Victorian tale-teller, even in the earlier stories. The sense of extreme suffering at the end of book 5 of *The Return of the Native* is created as much by the self-awareness of Clym and Eustacia as by the portentous descriptions of them and of Egdon Heath. It is Tess's unwavering determination to be true to her own nature, even during her moments of license and indecision, that makes the reader accept the tragic ponderings contributed by the narrator to Tess's story. But the effect of dramatic — that is, objective — establishment of mood in these novels is muted by the reminders in *The Return of the Native* that Clym and Eustacia are shadowy symbols of dimly conceived aspects of the universal situation and by the presence in *Tess of the d'Urbervilles* of a commentator who points out that Tess's guilt feelings are not supported by any genuinely valid morality. So in *Jude the Obscure* one is prepared to encounter a dramatic presentation, but it comes as something of a surprise that the presentation is almost entirely dramatic. There is of course a narrator to describe the events; Hardy no more than James could dispense with an entity to describe physical actions in a third-person story. But the narrator seldom utters as his own the pronouncements, the philosophizings, the interpretation of concatenated events that are hallmarks of the supposedly didactic quality of *Jude the Obscure*. (When the narrator does comment in his own voice, that voice is dissociated from the context in a manner that undercuts the narrator's authoritativeness.)

The narrator of *Jude the Obscure* expresses several interpretations of events and life, but he makes clear that he is either describing or rendering the opinion of one or more of the characters. The opinions are temporal, dependent upon the immediate situation. For instance, Jude often condemns the way the universe and society are organized when the dreams and ideals of his finer nature are frustrated by the actual conditions of his life. After Sue weds Phillotson, Jude first indulges in the wild hope that she will come back to him that evening. But he then decides that it "was a new beginning of Sue's history," and he idealizes his love for her:

> He projected his mind into the future, and saw her with children more or less in her own likeness around her. But the consolation of regarding them as a continuation of her identity was denied to him, *as to all such dreamers*, by the wilfulness of Nature in not allowing issue from one parent alone. Every desired renewal of an existence is debased by being half alloy. "If at the estrangement or death of my lost love, I could go and see her child—hers solely—there would be comfort in it!" said Jude. And then he again uneasily saw, as he had latterly seen with more and more frequency, the scorn of Nature for man's finer emotions, and her lack of interest in his aspirations. [P. 212: my italics]

The probability that this was also Hardy's own response to the death in 1890 of his youthful love, Tryphena Sparks (see "To a Motherless Child"), does not lessen the specific applicability to Jude's state of mind in the aftermath of losing Sue.

Another passage of this sort occurs after Jude first kisses the married but unhappy Sue. Jude realizes that his desire for her does not accord with his religious principles, and he wonders whether women are to blame that his aspiration has been checked again, as it had been by Arabella:

> Strange that his first aspiration—towards academical proficiency—had been checked by a woman, and that his second aspiration—towards apostleship—had also been checked by a woman. "Is it," he said, "that the women are to blame; or is it the artificial system of things, under which the normal sex-impulses are turned into devilish domestic gins and springes to noose and hold back those who want to progress?" [P. 261]

It can perhaps be assumed that this would be a serious question to Hardy, even though he might not be able to offer a single resolution. Not only does the use of quotation marks clearly make this a dra-

matic statement but a subsequent remark, given through Jude's
consciousness, also suggests his awareness of the limitations of his
questioning: "It was not for him to consider further: he had only to
confront the obvious, which was that he had made himself quite an
imposter as a law-abiding religious teacher" (p. 261).

I have already mentioned the scene in which Jude finds "nature's logic" to be "horrid." Another early scene also helps establish
Jude's point of view as individualistic within the novel; only someone
very willing to be persuaded could believe that the youthful Jude presents the adult attitudes of a profoundly disillusioned Hardy. Jude
has admired Phillotson's ambition to go to Christminster to study
ancient tongues; and he decides that a knowledge of Latin and Greek
would be desirable. Failing to obtain any grammar books from the
peddler Physician Vilbert, Jude writes to Phillotson, and eagerly opens
the parcel from Christminster that will grant him ready entrance to
all the learned secrets. He assumes that there is a "rule, prescription,
or clue of the nature of a secret cipher, which, once known, would
enable him, by merely applying it, to change at will all words of his
own speech into those of the foreign one" (p. 30). Jude is amazed and
downcast to discover upon opening the grammars that there is no
"law of transmutation" and that, rather, he would have to commit to
memory "at the cost of years of plodding...every word in both Latin
and Greek." Jude's reaction is strong: he thinks his high hopes were a
"grand delusion," and he wishes that "he had never seen a book, that
he might never see another, that he had never been born" (p. 31). The
exaggeration in these views is the clue that Hardy, contrary to general
critical opinion, is capable of an ironic presentation of ideas that in
essence parallel his own. Jude does in the matter of a month or two
return to the grammars, "grown callous to the shabby trick played
him by the dead languages." Indeed, the "herculean" labor required
to learn languages "gradually led him on to a greater interest in it than
in the presupposed patent process" (p. 33). In both situations — in
Farmer Troutham's field and with his hope of easy classical learning
— it is Jude's personality that causes his reaction, not Hardy's obtru-
siveness. The narrator's voice in itself is mocking: "shabby trick
played him by the dead languages."

Between these two descriptions of Jude's state of mind concerning classical studies appears one of the passages most frequently

quoted to illustrate Hardy's own bleak view of the universe:

> Somebody might have come along that way who would have asked
> [Jude] his trouble, and might have cheered him by saying that his no-
> tions were further advanced than those of his grammarian. But *nobody
> did come, because nobody does*; and under the crushing recognition of
> his *gigantic* error Jude continued to wish himself out of the world.
> [Pp. 31-32; my italics]

Analyzing this passage in its context requires considerable revision of
the reading that accepts it as Hardy's personal view.[12] Of course, to
see it in context does not make it mean the reverse of what most
readers have taken it to mean. It is still the expression of the grimness
of man's situation. However, it is no longer Hardy's expression, but
that of a naive boy. Perhaps most important as a modification of the
usual reading, the grimness is proved to be irrelevant; Jude's disillusion does not damage him. He quickly (given the pace of rural life)
sets himself to learning the difficult languages amid unpromising circumstances, studying while driving a bakery cart. If indeed it is "true"
that "no one comes," it is a good thing; for Jude develops independence and perseverance.

Another often quoted passage is important because it teeters
on the edge of authorial intrusion. Again, however, it shows not a
philosophical position of Hardy's but an attitude of Jude's that is mani-
festly incomplete and illogical. Jude marries Arabella because he
thinks she is pregnant. When she reveals that she is not, it becomes
evident that Jude's complaints about marriage and sex are based more
on selfish vanity and on a narrow perspective than on an adequately
based urge to a profound rebellion.

> There seemed to him, vaguely and dimly, something wrong in a social
> ritual which made necessary a cancelling of well-formed schemes in-
> volving years of thought and labour, of foregoing a man's one oppor-
> tunity of showing himself superior to the lower animals, and of con-
> tributing his units of work to the general progress of his generation,
> because of a momentary surprise by a new and transitory instinct which
> had nothing in it of the nature of vice, and could be only at the most
> called weakness. He was inclined to inquire what he had done, or she
> lost, for that matter, that he deserved to be caught in a gin which would
> cripple him, if not her also, for the rest of a lifetime? There was per-

haps something fortunate in the fact that the immediate reason of his marriage had proved to be non-existent. But the marriage remained. [Pp. 70-71]

Jude in this rumination ignores (because, as he says, they no longer exist) the actual reasons for his marriage: Arabella's pregnancy, and the economic necessity that a father support his children. Although the passage is preceded by a rhetorical question about prevailing "ordinary notions" that forced Jude to act as he did ("But how came they to prevail?"), Jude in the passage itself is quite obviously forgetting the "notion" about paternity and thinking only of the "notion" of reparation for seduction ("what . . . she [had] lost"). Readers who take this passage as expressing Hardy's rebellion against idealistic sexual mores overlook the fact that Jude felt no compunction about leaving the deflowered Arabella to pursue his ambition to go to Christminster; he stays and marries her only because he thinks she is pregnant. Neither Jude nor Arabella gives any thought to reparation for lost virginity until this passage, in which Jude pities himself for being married and prefers to construct an obviously canting social law he can blame rather than probe more deeply into his wife's "mistake" in thinking she had been pregnant. The uncertainty about which moral criteria are being condemned here is consistent with Jude's bleak theorizing in characteristic fashion upon the destruction of an ideal. Throughout the novel Jude shows a reluctance to face up to conditions that are not in accord with his mental and emotional state. (There is certainly no reason to doubt that this passage represents Hardy's view as to the moral unimportance of virginity. But the grammatical logic of the paragraph forces us to take the ideas to be Jude's. The very clause "there seemed to him" clearly locates the idea within the consciousness of Jude, who characteristically again reacts slowly — and, at this stage, impercipiently — to another of life's lessons.)

A passage similar to this in technique is unquestionably dramatic in function, since it is a direct statement by Sue. Jude and Sue, who are in Marygreen for the burial of their aunt shortly after Sue's marriage, confess their affection for each other, and Sue refers to her personal experience as a justification for divorce:

"Jude, before I married him I had never thought out fully what marriage meant, even though I knew. It was idiotic of me—there is no excuse. I was old enough, and I thought I was very experienced. So I rushed on, when I had got into that Training School scrape, with all the cock-sureness of the fool that I was! . . . I am certain one ought to be allowed to undo what one has done so ignorantly! I daresay it happens to lots of women: only they submit, and I kick." [P. 258]

Because precisely what Sue "had never thought out" and what she "knew" are ambiguous, one cannot say there is massive self-contradiction in her claim that she has married Phillotson "ignorantly." But Sue's dilemma, of a piece with her doubling back upon her own opinions which early and late in the novel causes Jude most of his misery, claims something less than clear sympathy. Hardy, in making a torn person like Sue a spokesman for a view he had much sympathy with, prevents what might easily in lesser hands have been dogmatism.[13]

*Jude the Obscure* contains a number of similar ironic comments, and extreme statements with little cause, showing that Hardy was detached from the fiction he was organizing (or, as he wrote to Gosse, allowing to organize itself). As if in witty self-parody, the narrator describes the "predestinate Jude" violating his resolute effort to study one Sunday in order that he might visit Arabella: *"Foreseeing* such an event he had already arrayed himself in his best clothes" (p. 48; my italics). A more elaborate instance of irony follows Jude's confronting Arabella with the knowledge that he knows where she learned how to ensnare him. Laughing coldly, she says:

"Every woman has a right to do such as that. The risk is hers."
"I quite deny it, Bella. She might if no life-long penalty attached to it for the man, or, in his default, for herself; if the weakness of the moment could end with the moment, or even with the year. But when effects stretch so far she should not go and do that which entraps a man if he is honest, or herself if he is otherwise."
"What ought I to have done?"
"Given me time. . . . Why do you fuss yourself about melting down that pig's fat to-night? Please put it away!"
"Then I must do it to-morrow morning. It won't keep."
"Very well—do." [P. 78]

Irony is at two points here. First, if Arabella had given Jude time, he would have gone to Christminster, as he makes clear a few pages earlier (pt. 1, chap. 9), and she would have lost him. Second, if the final interchange (which concludes the chapter) means anything at all, it is that Jude's irritation with Arabella's seducing him away from his dream has not diminished her desirability, for the implication of Jude's last speech, which logically can be read only as a command to Arabella to render the pig's fat in the morning, is that they will now go to bed together. Another example of irony opens part 3 and reflects on Jude's desire to become a licentiate in the Church. The use of point of view here, if a trifle unsubtle, is detached in the manner of James. Jude initially recognizes that his former desire to be a bishop had been the product of "mundane ambition masquerading in a surplice." He then proceeds to ponder delightedly on a career in which he could not rise higher than a humble curacy in an "obscure village or city slum — that might have a touch of goodness and greatness in it; that might be true religion, and a purgatorial course worthy of being followed by a remorseful man" (p. 153). The pious vanity in Jude's prospective career as a licentiate is evidence of the slowness of his evolution toward comprehension of his self and of the value of human endeavor.

A major irony of the novel involves Sue and Jude's reluctance to marry each other after their divorces from their first marriages are final. She shrinks from marriage with Jude because marriage is "irrevocable." It is starkly inconsistent for Sue to call marriage an "iron contract" (p. 311) when she and Jude have just remarked on how easy it is for a poor person to obtain a divorce. Moreover, her diatribe here is against government for licensing love (p. 312), not against society for restraining divorce.

The context of philosophical remarks usually reveals that authorial distance is maintained. The reflection that it is a "fundamental error" to base a permanent contract like marriage on a "temporary feeling which had no necessary connection with affinities that alone render a life-long comradeship tolerable" is Jude's (p. 80), although Hardy, contributing to a symposium a decade later, said approximately the same thing. The belief that *real* life is not to be found in universities and studies is stated by Sue (p. 180) and, more centrally, by Jude after he receives the discouraging reply to his request for advice from one of the dons (p. 139). The bitter declaration that "cruelty is the law prevading all nature and society; and we can't get out of it if we would!" (p. 384) is made by Phillotson to Arabella after she has tormented him with the advice that he should not have been so lenient with Sue as to accept her qualms about marital relations. Even the symbolic meanings of Father Time are usually presented by means of another character's consciousness: it is the grief-stricken Sue who perceives upon looking at his corpse that he is the "nodal point" of "all the inauspiciousness and shadow which had darkened the first union of Jude, and all the accidents, mistakes, fears, errors of the last" (p. 406); and Jude repeats the doctor's belief that Father Time's homicide and suicide are "the beginning of the coming universal wish not to live" (p. 406).

# III

The narrative distance that is created by irony does not always function to advance characterization as clearly as in those passages discussed above. In some instances, irony is used by the narrator speaking in his own voice instead of filtering opinions through characters. What is one to make of the robin, for example, which examines the preparations for the pig-killing and flies away, "not liking the sinister look of the scene" (p. 73)? Is this gratuitous animism, or is Hardy implying the similarities between man and animal (both, of course, to be pitied) as he had between sensate and insensate nature in *The Woodlanders*? And what about the image of Farmer Troutham punishing Jude for letting the rooks eat the corn, the sound of the clacker "echoing from the brand-new church tower just behind the mist, towards the building of which structure the farmer had largely subscribed, to testify his love for God and man" (p. 12)? If this is meant as a serious attack upon Troutham, Hardy is challenging the necessary functions of agriculture, which, it is obvious, the other Wessex novels support abundantly. That he was struck with a bird-clacker, presumably on the buttocks, might be painful to Jude, but that he was caused pain would scarcely seem to justify the marshalling of the forces of humanity and religious feeling against Troutham.

It seems to me that these ironies perform a larger function than simple reflections upon the incident at hand. They create a situation, by calling for a reaction more intense than the scenes require, which would in other novelists' work be termed sentimentalism. The nature of sentimentalism enjoins a special narrator-narrative relationship, in which the narrator reacts, and tries to make his render react, in a way not necessitated by his materials. The same sentimental function is fulfilled, I believe, in other Wessex novels, but not in so large a way as in *Jude the Obscure.*

Hardy's narrative voice is close to sentimentalism throughout the novel; it might reasonably be thought that deviations from strict objectivity in the perspective of his narrator, such as the above, give support to those critics who consider *Jude the Obscure* propaganda more than art. And indeed there is no way finally and absolutely to combat this judgment. There is little value in arguing that *Jude the Obscure* — or any work of art — is completely under the conscious control of its maker. But while allowing for an occasional or even a serious lapse,[14]   the weight of the evidence is that Hardy's sustaining effort was to make the novel a dramatic, or objective, expression of ideas, not all of which he held himself. His sense of artistic distance comprehends the use of the obtrusive narrator in such a manner that the narrator does not gain a uniquely authoritative stature. When the narrator stands apart from the narrative, it is sometimes because the action within the narrative does not substantiate his commentary, and sometimes because the narrator's judgments in particular contexts go contrary to his judgments in other contexts. Hardy-as-narrator may enter the story, but his entrance does not invalidate the concrete evidences of the story nor do the concrete evidences of the story invalidate the narrator's function. But they do prevent the narrator from gaining an aura of omniscience, and his judgments have no greater authority than those of the characters.[15]

The effect of employing the narrator in the manner of another character with a limited or special point of view can be examined through a few representative passages. The first passage is distinguished by the presence of a commentary that exceeds the requirements of the scene; the other passages show the narrator susceptible to the appeal of particular contexts, even though his responses to the appeals constitute self-contradiction.

When Sue does not return to her dormitory at the Teachers'

College, the other girls talk about the unlikelihood that Jude is actually Sue's cousin, as she had claimed. The girls, or at least some of them, gain vicarious excitement at the idea "of being kissed by such a kindly-faced young man." When they retire to their beds, the narrator muses for a paragraph upon the situation of women in nature, before the objective reportorial narrative resumes:

> Half-an-hour later they all lay in their cubicles, their tender feminine faces upturned to the flaring gas-jets which at intervals stretched down the long dormitories, every face bearing the legend "The Weaker" upon it, as the penalty of the sex wherein they were moulded, which by no possible exertion of their willing hearts and abilities could be made strong while the inexorable laws of nature remain what they are. They formed a pretty, suggestive, pathetic sight, of whose pathos and beauty they were themselves unconscious, and would not discover till, amid the storms and strains of after-years, with their injustice, loneliness, child-bearing, and bereavement, their minds would revert to this experience as to something which had been allowed to slip past them insufficiently regarded.
>
> One of the mistresses came in to turn out the lights, and before doing so gave a final glance at Sue's cot, which remained empty. [P. 168]

The lament about the future woe of the young girls is inserted arbitrarily, that is, not required by the conditions of the story. Since it is a detached comment, irrelevant in context, it is "sentimental" in Hardy's unique manner. The narrator interprets more than the situation warrants. The lament thus has the striking effect of remaining suspended beyond the narrative, characterizing its enunciator as having an ingrained bias that colors his interpretation of experience.

Other narrator commentary — such as that on the brief duration of romantic love in marriage (pp. 65-66), or on the animosity of contemporary logic toward what Jude holds in reverence (pp. 98-99) — has much the same tone as that which describes the fate of women. Such commentary, in that it conveys the inadequacy of the protagonists' grasp of life's principles and in that it seldom concretely substantiates the generalizations it voices, increases authorial distance. [16]

Two instances will suffice to clarify the nature of the narrator's self-contradictoriness. After Sue and Jude first kiss passionately, just before Sue returns to Phillotson after attending her aunt's funeral in Marygreen, the narrator analyzes her state of mind:

Then the slim little wife of a husband whose person was disagreeable to her, the ethereal, fine-nerved, sensitive girl, quite unfitted by temperament and instinct to fulfil the conditions of the matrimonial relation with Phillotson, *possibly with scarce any man,* walked fitfully along, and panted, and brought weariness into her eyes by gazing and worrying hopelessly. [P. 263; my italics]

The narrator shows in the italicized words a temporal perspective as limited as that of any human character. Sue may be fastidious and she may have underdeveloped sexual instincts, but as the narrator states elsewhere in the novel, Jude *and Sue* are happy (pp. 328, 372; see p. 377 for Sue's testimony). And Sue does exhibit sexual passion in a variety of circumstances—for example, when she finally capitulates to Jude (pp. 321-22), during his last visit to her after she has rejoined Phillotson (pp. 470-71), and when she declares to Mrs. Edlin that she loves Jude "O, grossly!" (p. 476). It is certainly more reasonable to believe that she does have a degree of genuine sexual passion than to believe—as now seems the fashionable critical approach— that all of these indications are efforts on Sue's part to disguise her sexlessness by pretending to have "conventional" sexual feelings. Moreover, from the time Sue and Jude finally begin sexual relations (p. 321) to her revulsion upon the death of her children (p. 415), she is not coquettish and tormenting, but as orthodox a helpmate as any in Victorian fiction. The only "condition" of the "matrimonial relation" that she is unfitted to fulfill is its coerciveness. But the context of this passage (p. 263)—it immediately follows Jude and Sue's passionate parting kiss—makes it clear that the narrator's concern is for Sue's physical revulsion from Phillotson, which causes her to sleep that night in a clothes closet (p. 265), a revulsion that several times is strongly hinted to be a personal reaction to Phillotson (for example, see pp. 476-77).

The final passage to be considered shows the narrator with a unique perspective and occurs during Jude and Sue's walk in the fields after they learn that they have both been divorced by their spouses and thus are free to marry each other:

They rambled out of the town, and along a path over the low-lying lands that bordered it, though these were frosty now, and the extensive seed-fields were bare of colour and produce. The pair, however, were so absorbed in their own situation that their surroundings were little in their consciousness. [P. 311]

Now, the love of Jude and Sue at this point has not been consummated. The field in which they are walking symbolizes their barren state, with the correspondence of emotion and scene common in Hardy's works (see *Tess of the d'Urbervilles,* p. 190). But as is appropriate for each of their individual consciousnesses, they pay no notice. The narrator, then, supplies for the reader a standard of judgment or a moral tonality. The morality is contradictory to that which is implicit in the description of the girls in their dormitory beds. There, female life was seen as rigorous, mainly because of their future cursed maternal role; here, life without reproduction is cold and wasted. I am consciously pushing the symbolic import of the coldness of the landscape, but only to emphasize the essential point, namely, the contrast in narrator moralities.

## IV

A pervasive relativism results from the complexity of perspectives. To say that relativism is the dominant narrative mode of a story that is usually described as doctrinaire, even "preachy," is not so iconoclastic as may first seem. For one of the main "doctrines" of the novel is precisely that opinion on a matter depends upon the point of view from which it is surveyed. After Jude returns from his first Sunday evening walk with Arabella, when he had kissed her, his attitude toward his studies has undergone alteration:

> He walked as if he felt himself to be another man from the Jude of yesterday. What were his books to him? what were his intentions, hitherto adhered to so strictly, as to not wasting a single minute of time day by day? "Wasting!" It depended on your point of view to define that: he was just living for the first time: not wasting life. It was better to love a woman than to be a graduate, or a parson; ay, or a pope! [P. 53]

Shortly after this scene, emphasis is again given to the relativity of perspective in judgment. Jude, loathing the necessity to kill the pig that Arabella has fattened, accidentally kicks over the pail of pig's blood.

> Jude put the pail upright, but only about a third of the whole steaming liquid was left in it, the main part being splashed over the snow, and forming a dismal, sordid, ugly spectacle — to those who saw it as other than an ordinary obtaining of meat. [P. 75]

The narrative perspective in each of these scenes is Jude's (though less certainly in the second), but nothing by the narrator proper contradicts the concept of relativism that the scenes enunciate. And Jude himself is aware of the poles of judgment that might be made upon his attitudes:

> Jude felt dissatisfied with himself as a man at what he had done [killing the pig quickly instead of slowly] , though aware of his lack of common sense, and that the deed would have amounted to the same thing if carried out by deputy. The white snow, stained with the blood of his fellow-mortal, wore an illogical look to him as a lover of justice, not to say a Christian: but he could not see how the matter was to be mended. No doubt he was, as his wife had called him, a tender-hearted fool. [P. 76]

The relative validity of the several viewpoints of the characters and the narrator is supported by the lack of absolutes in the story. In addition to the above passages, those dealing with Mrs. Edlin and Gillingham are central to this aspect of the novel. Indeed, the main function these minor characters perform is to underline the necessity of judgments appropriate to immediate chronological times, and the illegitimacy of dogmatic set notions of any origin. Gillingham's first appearance is as the spokesman for conventional society. Approached by Phillotson, who wants to explain why he is allowing his wife to live with Jude, Gillingham's reflection to himself is, "I think she ought to be smacked, and brought to her senses — that's what I think!" (p. 280). He advises Phillotson to resign his position at the school to avoid the scandal of a public hearing that would prevent him from obtaining a position at another good school (p. 298).[17]  He subsequently gives less orthodox advice when Phillotson asks his

views about the advisability of allowing Sue to come back. "Gillingham replied, naturally, that now she was gone it were best to let her
be; and considered that if she were anybody's wife she was the wife
of the man to whom she had borne three children and owed such trag-
ical adventures"; besides, they would probably marry in good time,
"and all would be well, and decent, and in order" (p. 433). When Sue
has returned to Phillotson, Gillingham reverses position again, and
says that Phillotson should never have let her go in the first place
because it had ruined his career; but he also shrewdly observes to
himself that "the reactionary spirit induced by the world's sneers and
his own physical wishes would make Phillotson more orthodoxly
cruel to her than he had erstwhile been informally and perversely
kind" (pp. 442-43). Although not a pivotal character in his own right,
Gillingham perceives the ambivalence of situation: he recognizes the
painfulness of Sue's position and the onerousness of Phillotson's; he
is impressed by Sue as a person and sympathizes with her for Phillotson's inept (as he would look at it) handling of her in the past; but he
continues to support her remarriage to Phillotson.

Mrs. Edlin opposes Gillingham's ideas of social decorum by her
forthright acceptance of individuality: she has no moral or social objection to Sue and Jude's not marrying after their divorces from Phillotson and  Arabella. But she parallels Gillingham's function as a
counterbalance to Sue and Jude's attitude toward marriage. She twice
scornfully contrasts the present-day obsessive, shrinking fear
of marrying with her own generation's fear of war and hunger (pp.
346, 444). She and her "poor man . . . thought no more o't than of a
game o' dibs"—they spent their wedding week reveling and began
their housekeeping with a borrowed half-crown; Jude and Sue fear to
marry because the "coercion" implicit in the marriage bond may kill
their love. She observes at Sue's second wedding to Phillotson, "Wed-
dings be funerals 'a b'lieve nowadays. . . . Times have changed since
then [when she was married]!" (p. 481). In brief, philosophizing in
the novel is mainly anti-marriage, presented in a way that gains the
reader's sympathy; but Hardy also presents opposite opinions, from
an older generation, to suggest that Jude and Sue see only halters on
ethereality and perfection when there exist more pertinent material
limitations on happiness.

Relativism is enhanced by an aspect of the Wessex novels that

is generally thought not to apply to *Jude the Obscure*.[18]   In most of
Hardy's novels, association with the soil and with the past gives his
rural characters sustenance. Jude and Sue do not tap this sustaining
source; but their failure to do so does not mean that the source is no
longer present. They simply do not take advantage of its existence,
or are incapable of reacting to it as long as they try to make their
lives in the modern world of change and mobility. That the authority
of Wessex soil has not been dissipated totally is made unmistakable
early in the novel. The distance between Jude and the narrator is
never more clearly communicated than in Jude's reaction to Farmer
Troutham's field:

> "How ugly it is here!" he murmured.
>     The fresh harrow-lines seemed to stretch like the channellings in
> a piece of new corduroy, lending a meanly utilitarian air to the expanse,
> taking away its gradations, and depriving it of all history beyond that of
> the few recent months, though to every clod and stone there really at-
> tached associations enough and to spare — echoes of songs from
> ancient harvest-days, of spoken words, and of sturdy deeds. Every inch
> of ground had been the site, first or last, of energy, gaiety, horse-play,
> bickerings, weariness. Groups of gleaners had squatted in the sun on
> every square yard. Love-matches that had populated the adjoining ham-
> let had been made up there between reaping and carrying. Under the
> hedge which divided the field from a distant plantation girls had given
> themselves to lovers who would not turn their heads to look at them by
> the next harvest; and in that ancient cornfield many a man had made
> love-promises to a woman at whose voice he had trembled by the next
> seed-time after fulfilling them in the church adjoining. *But this neither
> Jude nor the rooks around him considered.* For them it was a lonely
> place, possessing, in the one view, only the quality of a work-ground,
> and in the other that of a granary good to feed in. [P. 10; my italics]

Obviously, the land in Marygreen has plenty of associations — indeed,
a superfluity of them, as if Hardy is underlining a point. But Jude,
though a boy from the rural community of Mellstock (Hardy's name
for his childhood parish), does not appreciate the land. He may be
deracinated, but deracination is not the necessary condition. A peasant mode of life goes on in Marygreen not greatly different from
that in *Far from the Madding Crowd* or *The Return of the Native,*
except in the amount of space given to its portrayal. The carter who
tells Jude about Christminster is content with his original place in

life; he says that to "raise" ministers is "their business, like anybody else's" (p. 23); and the other Marygreen inhabitants who have been to Christminster think of it as a very slow place indeed (p. 133). There is an achievable, if attenuated, world of peace whose inhabitants do not suffer from uneasy aspiration in *Jude the Obscure,* just as in *The Return of the Native* or *Far from the Madding Crowd*; but Jude like the early Clym does not heed the demands of that world nor exploit its opportunities for repose and acquiescence. On his aunt's first casual statement that Phillotson should have taken Jude to Christminster with him, Jude considers leaving the rural community (p. 14). And although he lives there for a decade and a half, he never gains a sense of community, never shares in the lives of his fellows. When he revisits Marygreen with Sue, his associations are all personal (pp. 227-28), an indication that he had not taken the trouble to absorb the traditions and customs of the locality (admittedly difficult in face of the modernizing changes that had taken place in the hamlet [p. 6] ). His inability to develop and maintain a sustaining awareness of his role within a society is amplified in his posture toward Christminster. His feelings for the university and cathedral city are almost entirely intellectual and abstract rather than those which would allow him the sense of mutual interrelatedness that makes the peasants content with the lot given them in life. Indeed, Jude is hard put to maintain even his limited sense of association with Christminster. After Sue's marriage, "the City of learning wore an estranged look, and he had lost all feeling for its associations" (p. 213); and throughout the novel he is struck more by the recollections of long dead or departed Christminster students, with whose shades his imagination populates the streets, than he is with the actual physical existence of the on-going activities of the town. Even his occasional participation in the "real" life of Christminster, when he drinks and blasphemes in the tavern, is more a reaction against his frustrated idealisms than a response to the nature of the town itself; and his memories of those moments of participation shame or anger him rather than develop his sense of community.

Sue, also, has no sense of the unity of lives, and gains no strength from associations. She objects to an old house in which she and Phillotson live because "I feel crushed into the earth by the weight of so many previous lives there spent" (p. 243). The alien-

ation of Jude and Sue from an *available* source of power adds to the
pervading sense of tragedy, which, indeed, looms over the novel partially because the main characters are unable to be content with peas-
antlike acceptance. There is no conclusive evidence that the source
of peasant strength has vanished; but the protagonists have moved
away from it, into a more complex world where the simple patterns
are no longer applicable.


## V


The distance that Hardy places between himself and his narrator, and
between his narrator and the characters, permits a shift in the method
of presentation of tragedy toward the end of the novel. The point of
view becomes generally detached and objective. The characterization
and action are carried on in dialogue. To a large measure, the narrator ceases to function as another character interjecting interpretive
remarks. He becomes the reporter of events; once Hardy has set up
the possibilities of relativism through the use of complex characters
and a multiplicity of interpretive angles, he lets the material work
itself out dramatically, much as he does in *The Return of the Native.*
A very expressive "philosophical" scene in the novel is Jude's declaration of disillusionment but not defeat at the Remembrance Day festi-
vities at Christminster. The·long speech, sketchily prepared in his
characteristic way and with the occasion developing abruptly, fits
in with all the characterizations we have seen of Jude, both externally and by self-analysis. He is not "right" in this speech: he is true
to himself. Since he has to a large degree shifted positions with Sue,
he is in "a chaos of principles — groping in the dark — acting by instinct and not after example." He is dejected at not having come to
more solid ground, but he does not falsify the tentativeness of his
insight. "I perceive there is something wrong somewhere in our social
formulas: what it is can only be discovered by men or women with
greater insight than mine, — if, indeed, they ever discover it — at least
in our time" (p. 394). The reader, now accustomed to short-lived intellectual stands, does not expect Jude to remain at the moral position
he maintains on Remembrance Day. Nor does he. At the end of the

novel, again reacting from disillusion and personal despair, and from Sue's abandonment of him for Phillotson, he goes beyond principled tentativeness to choose death. His mournful deathbed motto—*"Let the day perish wherein I was born, and the night in which it was said, There is a man child conceived"* (p. 488) — marks a different personality from the boy who upon being discharged by Troutham perceived "his existence to be an undemanded one" (p. 15), and who upon learning the difficulty of Latin and Greek grammar "continued to wish himself out of the world" (p. 32). Much of Jude's early, largely self-imposed suffering is unpersuasive; but by the end of the novel Hardy's methods of objectifying the narrator have justified his hope, expressed in the 1912 postscript to the preface, that *Jude the Obscure* contains tragic qualities.

The alternation of views among the narrator and the characters keeps allegiances in suspension, a factor important to the creation of tragedy by presenting no easy choices. Jude confronts basic and ultimate matters — the relation between the individual and a universe that seems to offer him no genuine freedom or opportunity for happiness — and he confronts those issues in a context that permits no answers. The novel is bleak for one reason because every alternative leads to another conjecture, another possibility. Jude seems to have no chance; yet the universe alone is not to blame. Jude could survive if he were not so totally an idealist and if he had not entrusted that idealism to a person so frail and inconsistent that, it can justly be said, Jude's choice of Sue is what dooms him. He admits he has cause for feeling better about the future — he declaims at Remembrance Day, and elsewhere, that his ambitions were ahead of his time; and he says that in fifty years people with his and Sue's inclination will be able to live together without needing religious sanction or legal contract. But these causes for eventual hope give him no personal sustenance. He fails because he has rested the making of answers to ultimate questions on the shoulders of the weakest of fellow humans. On the other hand, Jude's character is not solely to blame either. Jude has not been in error to love Sue; indeed, the drift of the entire novel is that they are like twins, parts of one person whose meeting and union are inevitable. Jude's destruction depends upon the interaction of a number of motives and external causes. In addition to those already alluded to, he has tried to combine intellectual attainment with his potential peasant resources, but instead of staying in a peasant community such as Marygreen where such a combination might be psychologically manageable, however scanty the opportunities to exercise one's intellectual attainments, Jude moves into an industrial society where neither intellectual aspiration nor peasant tradition has any value. Jude is distinguished by an impractical, idealizing intellect and a boundless ability to sympathize with the hopes and pains of others. It is his fate to have those particular qualities, which — when they confront the ambitions he acquires from his background and from Sue — lead to self-frustration and eventually self-destruction. He challenges the mysterious forces of the universe at the same instant that he tries to live by the most humane principles.

These suspended allegiances may point to what Hardy had in mind when he suggested that the novel might contain "cathartic, Aristotelian qualities" — beyond, of course, those Aristotelian features that are in almost all narratives, such as discovery and recognition scenes; and other than such matters as a protagonist of a social magnitude (which Jude certainly is not).[19] No matter how much we may sympathize with Sue and Jude, we recognize that they receive punishment fitting to the social norms they violate, even though they are morally superior to those norms. Through the difficulty of their lives Hardy makes the reader perceive that superiority; yet there is no injustice, for the mysterious forces that shape the conditions of life in Hardy's universe do not operate by laws of the accidental, whatever Jude may think (p. 413); they have selected for destruction exactly those persons whose outlook on life presents the gravest threat to their continued supremacy. Hardy's "gods" are as punctilious in their workings as those of Aeschylus and Sophocles. The reader and Hardy may feel that their operations are as thoughtless of individual worth and uniqueness of the protagonist's situation as are the forces that doom Oedipus. But like the justice that damns Oedipus for both his premeditated and his unpremeditated acts, the justice of *Jude the Obscure* works according to its own precepts. Threat or defiance toward the social law deserves no mercy. Had Jude been able to recant as Phillotson does, he might have saved himself; but like Oedipus, he refuses to cease his effort to lead an open life, to live by his principles. His unwavering truth to his sense of selfhood makes it impossible for him to become reconciled to conventional social wisdom, even though by the end of the novel his refusal costs him his life.

Hardy's turning to lyric, dramatic, and epic poetry after writing *Jude the Obscure* is a natural manner of exploiting the control and point of view which he had developed in fiction, especially in *Tess of the d'Urbervilles* and *Jude the Obscure*. The use of relativism, though it occurs in all of the novels, reaches new subtleties in *Jude the Obscure*. After taking it that far in fiction, Hardy continues to develop it in his poetry, in the use of what Samuel Hynes has called "anti-nomial patterns," to frame his themes.[20] And perhaps most important, recognition of the distancing effect of Hardy's presentation in *Jude the Obscure* makes clearer his meaning in his reflections upon his novel in the preface:

> Like former productions of this pen, *Jude the Obscure* is simply an endeavour to give shape and coherence to a series of seemings, or personal impressions, the question of their consistency or their discordance, of their permanence or their transitoriness, being regarded as not of the first moment. [P. viii]

The impressions may indeed be personal, but they are transmuted into universal suggestiveness and impersonal tentativeness by the methods that Hardy employs. Undogmatic impressions are the keystone of Hardy's art of the tragic. The final thrust of the novel, and indeed of all Hardy's tragic novels, is concisely expressed by William J. Hyde in his examination of different "levels of existence" sketched by Hardy in *Jude the Obscure*: "As a part, then, of their seeking the pattern of a higher and more spontaneous ethics, Hardy and [John Stuart] Mill appear markedly in favor of tolerating, indeed encouraging, unconventionality [ that is, honestly abiding by one's 'level of existence'] as a good in itself, for a healthy realization of individual human needs."[21]

\* \* \* \* \* \* \* \* \* \* \*

The separate formal characteristics of Hardy's novels have a common quality which unifies them. This unifying formal quality is Hardy's remarkably consistent, if sometimes awkwardly incorporated, refusal to take a stand on a philosophical or thematic issue in such a

way as to rely upon a justification outside the limitations of the world
of the particular novel. It is especially apparent in *Tess of the d'Urbervilles*, where the power is founded in the sanctity of the individual's
impressions and self-concept, and in *Jude the Obscure*, where point
of view is manipulated to objectify the narrator's opinions. But this
quality is present to a lesser or greater degree in all of the technical
devices this study has dealt with. The effectiveness of schematic
style and organization in *Far from the Madding Crowd* prevents
quick reader resolution of the subtleties of issues, even though the
novel as a whole is not tragic. The split allegiances that comprise
the form of *The Return of the Native* similarly prevent simplistic
resolutions of that novel's dilemmas about man's relationship to his
environment and to his society. The atomization of tragic qualities
among the several principal characters in *The Woodlanders* makes
that novel a stimulating experiment in form, preventing reader commitment to a single set of values. *The Mayor of Casterbridge* marks
an essential turning point in the evolution of this quality. In the
preceding novels this characteristic of Hardy's technique — its
exploratory nature that is open to tentativeness and even to self-
contradiction — appears in the style or the formulation of material,
that is, the technique affects the manner in which the ideas of the
novels are communicated. After *The Mayor of Casterbridge*, the
technique appears as a fundamental element inseparable from the
conception of reality within the novels. The atomization of tragic
qualities in *The Woodlanders* is a probative effort to get at the
classless, boundary-less nature of tragedy, which is given further
theoretical (as well as formal) justification in *Tess of the d'Urbervilles*, by the identification of tragic authority in the intensity of
individual consciousness. Hardy's last two novels, then, are less related to classical precepts of tragic example, and are less dependent
upon readers' literary expectations for their tragic effectiveness. Rather, the power of the last novels is communicated intrinsically through
their forms, which affirm that life is lived in uncertainty. Powerful
forces on all sides — and within the individual — present challenges
whose fearsomeness depends in part upon the impossibility that
the individual can know the ultimate worthiness of his antagonists,
or indeed of himself or of his own values.

   This shift in Hardy's impressionistic presentation of man's

dilemma places in sharper perspective the time-worn question, Can Hardy's last novels legitimately be called *tragic* with their lower-class protagonists and their pessimistic views of life? An examination of the effects of his forms has proved, I believe, what most readers have always felt, that the social class of the protagonists is irrelevant to the quality of the tragedy they can evoke; and a close notation of Hardy's stories reveals that there is no clear or predetermined course of the pessimism in the individual story, that Hardy attempts no final interpretation of man's efforts or sufferings. The customary classi-fication of Hardy's last novels as "naturalistic" is not necessarily in-correct; but it is misleading if it is intended to convey a judgment that such novels are a less valuable form of tragedy. Emphasis on the intensity and sanctity of individual perceptions in *Tess of the d'Urber-villes* and *Jude the Obscure* makes them among the most intimate and compelling narratives of the last century.

# NOTES

## CHAPTER ONE

1. Robert Schweik's closely argued analyses of various formal features in Hardy's novels constitute a marked exception to modern critics' indifference to Hardy's use of structure: "Theme, Character, and Perspective in Hardy's *The Return of the Native*," *PQ* 41 (1962): 757-67; "Moral Perspective in *Tess of the d'Urbervilles*," *CE* 24 (1962): 14-18; "Character and Fate in Hardy's *The Mayor of Casterbridge*," *NCF* 21 (1966): 249-62. Schweik's and my methods and conclusions sometimes differ; but as my chapter on *Tess of the d'Urbervilles* testifies, his ideas generate further ideas and development. Jean Brooks, *Thomas Hardy: The Poetic Structure* (Ithaca, N.Y.: Cornell Univ. Press, 1971), discusses such "poetic" structures as imagery, repetitions, and parallel situations.

2. Albert Guerard, *Thomas Hardy: The Novels and Stories* (Cambridge, Mass.: Harvard Univ. Press, 1949), p. 157.

3. Carl J. Weber, *Hardy of Wessex: His Life and Literary Career,* 2nd ed. (1st ed., 1940; New York: Columbia Univ. Press, 1965), p. 148.

4. Hardy, "The Profitable Reading of Fiction," *Forum* (New York), March

1888, pp. 57-70; reprinted in *Thomas Hardy's Personal Writings: Prefaces, Literary Opinions, and Reminiscences,* ed. Harold Orel (Lawrence: Univ. of Kansas Press, 1966), p. 121.

5. For a longer discussion of Hardy's views of realism and his anti-realistic aesthetics, see Morton Dauwen Zabel, "Hardy in Defense of His Art: The Aesthetic of Incongruity," *Craft and Character: Texts, Method, and Vocation in Modern Fiction* (New York: Viking, 1957), pp. 70-96; first printed in *Southern Review* 6 (1940): 125-49.

6. Preface to *The Dynasts,* pts. 1 and 2, Wessex ed. (London: Macmillan, 1913), vol. 2: verse.

7. Orel, p. 121.

8. Horace *De Arte Poetica* 40: "He who makes every effort to select his theme aright will be at no loss for choice words or lucid arrangement." From Edward Henry Blakeney, *Horace on the Art of Poetry* (London, 1928), p. 42; also Orel, p. 272.

9. Orel, pp. 122-23. For an excellent discussion of the functional simplicity of Hardy's style, see Benjamin Sankey, *The Major Novels of Thomas Hardy* (Denver: Alan Swallow, 1965), pp. 11-23.

10. Early critics of Hardy as tragedian in these terms are Lionel Johnson, *The Art of Thomas Hardy* (1894; reprinted, New York: Dodd, Mead, 1923), and Lascelles Abercrombie, *Thomas Hardy: A Critical Study* (London: Martin Secker, 1912). Critics who have continued in this initial reaction are Carl Weber, esp. in *Hardy of Wessex;* David Cecil, *Hardy the Novelist: An Essay in Criticism* (London: Constable, 1943); and Harvey Curtis Webster, *On a Darkling Plain, The Art and Thought of Thomas Hardy* (Chicago: Univ. of Chicago Press, 1947), and his letter to the editors of *VS* 4 (1960): 90-93.

11. Joseph Warren Beach, *The Technique of Thomas Hardy* (Chicago: Univ. of Chicago Press, 1922), pp. 94, 97.

12. For example, though David Cecil has warm admiration for Hardy, he pinpoints *Tess of the d'Urbervilles* and *Jude the Obscure* as failed tragedies for these reasons (pp. 132-33). See also F. R. Leavis, *The Great Tradition: George Eliot, Henry James, Joseph Conrad* (1st ed., 1948; London: Chatto & Windus, 1960), pp. 22-23; Frank Chapman, "Hardy the Novelist," *Scrutiny* 3 (1934): 22-37; Arthur Mizener, "The Novel of Doctrine in the Nineteenth Century: Hardy's *Jude the Obscure,*" *The Sense of Life in the Modern Novel* (Boston: Houghton Mifflin, 1964), pp. 55-77.

13. Krutch, *The Modern Temper* (New York: Harcourt, 1929), pp. 115-43.

14. Morrell (Kuala Lumpur: Univ. of Malaya Press, 1965).

15. Krutch, p. 138.

16. Ibid., p. 125.

17. William Van O'Connor, *Climates of Tragedy* (Baton Rouge: Louisiana State Univ. Press, 1943), p. 3.

18. Hardy's idea of free will is disputed and probably not possible to define conclusively. But a look at the view of John Stuart Mill, who after Darwin had the strongest lasting influence upon Hardy's ideas and phraseology, is instructive. In the *Autobiography* Mill compresses his opinion in order to state briefly the formative stages in his life:

> I perceived, that the word Necessity, as a name for the doctrine of Cause and Effect applied to human action, carried with it a misleading association; . . . I saw that though our character is formed by circumstances, our own desires can do much to shape those circumstances; and that what is really inspiriting and ennobling in the doctrine of freewill, is the *conviction that we have real power over the formation of our own character; that our will, by influencing some of our circumstances, can modify our future habits or capabilities of willing.* All this was entirely consistent with the doctrine of circumstances, or rather, was that doctrine itself, properly understood. From that time I drew, in my own mind, *a clear distinction between the doctrine of circumstances, and Fatalism;* discarding altogether the misleading word Necessity. The theory, which I now for the first time rightly apprehended, *ceased altogether to be discouraging,* and besides the relief to my spirits, I no longer suffered under the burthen, so heavy to one who aims at being a reformer in opinions, of thinking one doctrine true, and the contrary doctrine morally beneficial. [*Autobiography and Other Writings,* ed. Jack Stillinger, Riverside ed. (Boston: Houghton Mifflin, 1969), p. 102; my italics]

See also "Liberty and Necessity," in *The System of Logic,* and "Of Individuality," in *On Liberty,* for further discussions by Mill.

Since Hardy was also influenced by less benign observers of the limitations upon human choice, such as Matthew Arnold and Leopardi, one would not expect to find all features of Mill's definition of free will in Hardy's works. Nonetheless, the idea of "circumstances" in Hardy obviously loses some of its bleakness in the context of Mill's definition. Hardy's proud claim that he knew *On Liberty* "almost by heart" (*Later Years,* pp. 118-19) needs to be applied to his concept of free will as much as it does to his independence of thought; see Weber, *Hardy of Wessex* (1965), p. 41. Unlike Mill, Hardy did not give up the term, nor even the idea, of Necessity (see *Later Years,* p. 128), but in his conscious philosophy he also held to a limited free will at least until 1914 (*Later Years,* pp. 162, 165-66). After 1914, his remarks were more clearly deterministic (*Later Years,* pp. 271-73).

   In sum, it is probably wisest to avoid dogmatism about the degree or intensity of Hardy's belief in free will. He claimed to use "impressions" while writing, with no pretension that the totality of his impressions constituted a consistent philosophy. In the context of fiction's plotting and characterization, this leads to *de facto* free will and meaningful choice between alternatives that can be either well or ill understood by those who face the choice.

19. Henry Alonzo Myers, *Tragedy: A View of Life* (Ithaca, N.Y.: Cornell Univ. Press, 1956).

20. Sewall, *The Vision of Tragedy* (New Haven and London: Yale Univ. Press, 1959). Murray Krieger, *The Tragic Vision: Variations on a Theme in Literary Interpretation* (Chicago and London: Univ. of Chicago Press, 1960), published a year after Sewall's book, underscores the idea that tragedy contains precarious tension. Krieger says that the "tragic vision" (of the "abyss," that is, of the "existential absurdity of the moral life" [p. 15] ), is opposed by the "ethical vision" of an external or society-based moral code.

21. Sewall. p. 81; see also pp. 165-66, n85.

22. See Lionel Abel, "Is There a Tragic Sense of Life?" *Theater* 2; reprinted in *Moderns on Tragedy,* ed. Lionel Abel (New York: Fawcett, 1967), pp. 175-87. Abel says flatly that a tragic writer can have no formal philosophy (p. 186). Ian Gregor, "Hardy's World," *ELH* 38 (1971): 274-93, explores some techniques of philosophical impressionism based on "a series of seemings."

23. Sewall, p. 129.

24. See Sewall, p. 110.

25. See Dorothea Krook, *Elements of Tragedy* (New Haven and London: Yale Univ. Press, 1969), pp. 35-65. For further discussion of this point and for a denial that affirmation is a necessary effect of tragedy, see Walter Kaufmann, *Tragedy and Philosophy* (New York: Doubleday Anchor, 1969).

26. See John Paterson, "Hardy, Faulkner, and the Prosaics of Tragedy," *Cen-*

*tennial Review of Arts and Sciences* 5 (1961): 156-75, for a fuller discussion of stylistic differences that make Hardy's novels more successful as tragedies than Faulkner's. Bonamy Dobrée's analysis of the centrality of plot in creating the tragic mode is a broad and theoretic elucidation of Aristotle that substantiates Paterson's more detailed exploration; see his *The Lamp and the Lute* (Oxford: Clarendon Press, 1929), p. 31.

27. John Paterson, *"The Mayor of Casterbridge* as Tragedy," *VS* 3 (1959): 151-72; Webster's rejoinder is in the letter to the editors, *VS* 4 (1960): 90-93. Paterson, "The 'Poetics' of *The Return of the Native,*" *MFS* 6 (1960): 214-22, uses the same method of analysis in his reading of *The Return of the Native* as he does in *The Mayor of Casterbridge,* though he does not label *The Return of the Native* a tragedy. See also Helen Garwood, *Thomas Hardy: An Illustration of the Philosophy of Schopenhauer* (Philadelphia: John C. Winston, 1911), pp. 41-68.

28. Johnson, *The Art of Thomas Hardy*, pp. 42,48; Abercrombie, *Thomas Hardy*, p. 35.

## CHAPTER TWO

1. *The Spectator,* January 3, 1874.

2. For example, *The Observer,* January 3, 1875. Henry James, at the beginning of his life-long tepid response to Hardy's work, admitted it was "extremely clever," but disliked it because it lacked "magic" and "proportion." *Nation* (New York), December 24, 1874. These contemporary reviews are reprinted in *Thomas Hardy and His Readers,* ed. Laurence Lerner and John Holstrom (London: Bodley Head, 1968), pp. 23-38.

3. *Later Years,* p. 42: "Of course the book is all contrasts — or was meant to be in its original conception. Alas, what a miserable accomplishment it is, when I compare it with what I meant to make it! — *e.g.* Sue and her heathen gods set against Jude's reading the Greek testament; Christminster academical, Christminster in the slums; Jude the saint, Jude the sinner; Sue the Pagan, Sue the saint; marriage, no marriage; &c., &c."

4. James Wright, Afterword, *Far from the Madding Crowd,* Signet ed. (New York: New American Library, 1960), p. 378.

5. Guerard, *Thomas Hardy,* p. 68.

6. Richard C. Carpenter, "The Mirror and the Sword: Imagery in *Far from the Madding Crowd,*" *NCF* 18 (1964): 331-45.

7. Bathsheba is accused of unnatural behavior by certain characters. Troy thinks there is something "abnormal" in a woman as independent as Bathsheba appealing with "childlike pain and simplicity" to be kissed also, after Troy has kissed the dead Fanny (p. 344); and Pennyways the discharged bailiff thinks her drinking cider through a straw not a "'nateral way at all'" (p. 417). But these references to "unnaturalness" characterize the perversities of the speakers more than those of Bathsheba.

8. See Guerard's listing of developmental character traits that affect heroines in successive novels, for example, Marty South and Suke Damson in *The Woodlanders* being "combined" to form Tess Durbeyfield (*Thomas Hardy,* pp. 141-42). Still, the configuration is different for each individual.

9. George Wing, *Hardy* (Edinburgh: Oliver and Boyd, 1963), p. 52; Beach, *The Technique of Thomas Hardy,* pp. 49-50.

10. Richard C. Carpenter, *Thomas Hardy* (New York: Twayne, 1964), p. 87.

11. In fact, Hardy may go too far in the other direction. Some of the awkwardness in the final union of the protagonists would have been lessened if Hardy had not assured his readers, before Troy is killed, that Bathsheba finds it impossible to love Oak, or anyone (pp. 402, 410). It strikes me that Bathsheba is sincere on p. 410, that is, she does not have affection for Oak despite her irritation that he did not declare his own love when she asks his advice concerning Boldwood's proposal.

## CHAPTER THREE

1. In later life he was proud of having adhered to these unities in *The Return of the Native;* see *Early Life,* p. 160; *Later Years,* p. 235. See also my "Unity of Time in *The Return of the Native,*" *N & Q,* n.s. 12 (1965): 304-5.

2. For a comprehensive study of the traditional qualities and allusions in *The Return of the Native,* see Paterson, "The 'Poetics' of *The Return of the Native.*"

3. John Paterson's exploration of revisions in the manuscript, esp. those affecting the characterizations of Clym, Eustacia, and Diggory Venn, shows that Hardy had too many, conflicting notions and, because he had not resolved them before he began to write, he had a hard time doing so during the writing itself. *The Making of "The Return of the Native"* (Berkeley and Los Angeles: Univ. of California Press, 1960).

4. Previous readers have also defined their sense of conflicting sympathies

and idea-systems in the novel. See esp. Paterson, "The 'Poetics' of *The Return of the Native*," p. 215; Schweik, "Theme, Character, and Perspective in Hardy's *The Return of the Native*"; Robert W. Stallman, "Hardy's Hour-Glass Novel," *Sewanee Review* 55 (1947): 283-96; and Beach, *The Technique of Thomas Hardy*, p. 80.

5. An objection to my distinctions might be that Clym is as egoistic as Eustacia in his refusal to accede to her wishes to leave the heath. But the egoism and petty vanity of Eustacia's motivations do not correlate with the obstinacy and self-righteousness of Clym's. The very fact that they are unable to communicate to each other the simplest grounds for their individual determinations on this issue is an indication that they live and think on separate levels. An interesting essay whose insights are not fully developed, Richard Benvenuto's "Another Look at the Other Eustacia," *Novel* 4 (1970): 77-79, argues that Eustacia's only morality is individualism.

6. Whether Eustacia commits suicide or falls accidentally into the weir-pool is a perplexing issue for readers of Hardy. My assertion that she was a suicide is based on Hardy's "Sketch Map of the Scene of the Story," facing the title page of vol. 1 (London: Smith, Elder & Co., 1878), and upon a map plotting out the movements in the novel that I made before I saw Hardy's sketch. The most pertinent detail of the physical scene is that Eustacia's path from Mistover to the weir on the night of her death takes her across one road (and perhaps two; the road forks near the weir) just before she reaches the weir. Wildeve's coachlights should have been visible to her from this point in the road, and if she had been looking for Wildeve's coach she would have proceeded along the road instead of across it onto the meadow. Coupled with her last speeches of despair and her previous attempt to kill herself with her grandfather's pistols, these facts of the physical scene strike me as persuasive indications of suicide, though it is possible that in her distracted state of mind she did not notice the marked change in footing from the heath that a road would present. For a still more positive assertion that Eustacia was a suicide, see Ken Zellefrow, *"The Return of the Native*: Hardy's Map and Eustacia's Suicide," *NCF* 28 (1973): 214-20. Bruce K. Martin, "Whatever Happened to Eustacia Vye?" *Studies in the Novel* 4(1972): 619-27, summarizes other reasons to believe Eustacia was a suicide.

7. John Holloway, *The Victorian Sage: Studies in Argument* (London: Macmillan, 1953), p. 6, correlates these passages with Clym's finding a higher wisdom.

8. The best analysis of this general feeling is by Irving Howe, *Thomas Hardy* (New York: Macmillan, 1967), pp. 60-65. Howe accommodates the multiplicity of perspectives in the novel, acknowledging for example that Eus-

tacia is "like a young goddess of sensuality" as well as a "young girl of petulant vanity" (p. 65), and that the original conception of Clym as "dominated by modern deracination and a hunger for some nameless purpose" is a "triumph," but that Clym's actual presentation is "far too dim and recessive for the role Hardy assigns him" (p. 63). Robert Evans, "The Other Eustacia," *Novel* 1 (1968): 251-59, follows essentially Howe's criticism of Eustacia. A different stand is taken by David Eggenschwiler, "Eustacia Vye, Queen of Night and Courtly Pretender," *NCF* 25 (1971): 444-54; he believes that the split in the presentation of Eustacia is intentional, and that Eustacia is "both a genuinely tragic figure and a parody upon literary romanticism."

9. *Thomas Hardy*, p. 97.

10. See also Leonard Deen, "Heroism and Pathos in Hardy's *Return of the Native*," *NCF* 15 (1960): 207-19.

11. In context it is clear that Hardy is criticizing Eustacia's self-delusion; see M.A. Goldberg, "Hardy's Double-Visioned Universe," *EIC* 7 (1957): 378-82. Yet Hardy's own view as a young man was not too distant from Eustacia's: "*October 30th* [1870] . Mother's notion (and also mine) — that a figure stands in our van with arm uplifted, to knock us back from any pleasant prospect we indulge in as probable." *Thomas Hardy's Notebooks*, ed. Evelyn Hardy (London: Hogarth, 1955), p. 32.

12. An opposing viewpoint is that of J. Hillis Miller, who in *The Form of Victorian Fiction: Thackeray, Dickens, Trollope, George Eliot, Meredith, and Hardy* (Notre Dame, Ind.; Univ. of Notre Dame Press, 1968), rates Eustacia as the novel's only tragic actor because she gains "the detached vision of the futility of life which the narrator has had all along" (p. 117). Miller's point is appealing, since it implies that the novel finishes what it purportedly set out to do, and one would like to give in to one's own infatuation with and sympathy for Eustacia. But to make this point, Miller has to overlook the import of the frequent irony directed at Eustacia. Nor does he explain in what way Eustacia's ultimate "detached" vision, which allows her to "think what a sport for Heaven this woman Eustacia was," differs from her earlier anticipation that "Fate" will play a "cruel satire" upon her (*The Return of the Native*, pp. 403, 243). It is Miller's view that Hardy's characters lack effective free will and thus are not to blame for their fates; see his review of Roy Morrell, *Thomas Hardy: The Will and the Way*, in *VS* 10 (1967): 280-82, and Morrell's rejoinder in *VS* 11 (1967): 119-21. Taken together, of course, Miller's views are consistent: if mankind lacks free will except as "part of the irresistible movement of matter in its purposeless changes through time" (*VS* 10: 281), Eustacia's obsession with hostile chimeras ("creatures of her mind") is a justifiable response to her helplessness.

13. For a discussion of the request by the editor of *Belgravia* that Hardy alter the ending of *The Return of the Native*, see Weber, *Hardy of Wessex* (1965), pp. 106-7.


## CHAPTER FOUR

1. Republished in *Collected Poems* (London: Macmillan, 1930), p. 531.

2. "Candour in English Fiction," *New Review* 2 (1890): 16.

3. See *Our Exploits at West Poley*, ed. R.L. Purdy (New York: Oxford Univ. Press, 1952), p. 97, in which both "sense" and "energy" are needed for success. The Man who had Failed lacks "energy."

4. Norman Friedman argues this point in "Criticism and the Novel: Hardy, Hemingway, Crane, Woolf, Conrad," *Antioch Review* 18 (1958): 348-52. Friedman sometimes goes beyond his evidence, but his point is valid — that symbolic readings of fiction must supplement, not circumvent, the facts of the plot. *Studies in the Novel*, Thomas Hardy issue, contains two essays concerned with the relationship between Henchard's actions and his fate: Lawrence J. Starzyk, "Hardy's *Mayor*: The Antitraditional Basis of Tragedy," 4(1972):592-607; Duane D. Edwards, "*The Mayor of Caster-bridge* as Aeschylean Tragedy," 4(1972):608-18.

5. D.A. Dike, "A Modern Oedipus: *The Mayor of Casterbridge*," *EIC* 2 (1952): 177, suggests in passing that Farfrae will be challenged in his turn when "another sacrifice will be demanded." But Dike does not indicate that the inevitability of Farfrae's defeat lies in his character as surely as in the ritualistic pattern of the novel. The plausibility of the rendition of cyclic change in *The Mayor of Casterbridge* does not rely solely on classical mythic expectations. Julian Moynahan, "*The Mayor of Casterbridge* and the Old Testament's First Book of Samuel: A Study of Some Literary Rela-tionships," *PMLA* 71 (1956): 118-30, sees Farfrae and Henchard in relation to the biblical legend of David and Saul. See also John Holloway, "Hardy's Major Fiction," *From Jane Austen to Joseph Conrad* (Minneapolis: Univ. of Minnesota Press, 1958), pp. 241-42, who sees the conflict between Far-frae and Henchard as between a man and an animal; and Seymour Migdal, "History and Archetype in *The Mayor of Casterbridge*," *Studies in the Novel* 3 (1971):284-92, for whom the conflict is between two kinds of mentality.

6. John Paterson makes the same point about the men's moral standing at the end of the novel in "*The Mayor of Casterbridge* as Tragedy," pp. 157-

58. In his essay on the "prosaics" of tragedy, Paterson observes that the novel's "primitive rhythms" exploit "a fundamental process"—the contest between the old dispensation and the new ("Hardy, Faulkner, and the Prosaics of Tragedy," pp. 160-62). But in neither article does Paterson turn from Henchard in order to deal with Farfrae's role in this "process."

7. Two of these passages were added to the text after the serialization and the first edition: "that will make a hole in a sovereign" first appeared in the Sampson Low, Marston edition (London, 1887); "that he loved so well as never to have revisited it" first appeared in the Osgood, McIlvaine edition (London, 1895). That Hardy added these touches indicates a desire to emphasize his concept of Farfrae's character.

8. James F. Scott, "Spectacle and Symbol in Thomas Hardy's Fiction," *PQ* 44 (1965): 541, succinctly puts the view usually accepted of Hardy as artist: "He is totally unresponsive to the subtleties of point-of-view by which a writer such as James uses the perception of a particular character to invest an ordinary sight with symbolic significance." However, some recent criticism acknowledges Hardy's awareness and exploitation of point of view; see Audrey Charlotte Peterson, "Point of View in Thomas Hardy's *The Mayor of Casterbridge* and *Tess of the d'Urbervilles*" (Ph.D. diss., Univ. of Southern California, 1967), who makes some interesting observations despite a tendency to force ambiguous passages to coincide with her thesis. A more sophisticated essay is by Robert Kiely, "Vision and Viewpoint in *The Mayor of Casterbridge,*" *NCF* 23 (1968): 189-200.

9. In fact, Henchard by the end of the novel has gained qualities that would make him a challenger to Farfrae's position. But he has also achieved an insight into the worth of the world's prizes that disallows his making that challenge.

10. Hardy noted that James Payn, the reader for Smith, Elder & Co., told the publishing firm "that the lack of gentry among the characters made it uninteresting—a typical estimate of what was, or was supposed to be, mid-Victorian taste" (*Early Life*, pp. 235-36).

11. Though in terms of tragedy the townsmen's resentment toward Farfrae is the more significant, the novel's characters show perhaps greater verve in their attack on Lucetta. Nance Mockridge anticipates, by one page, Jopp's Aristotelianism in a humorous colloquial reference to Lucetta: "I do like to see the trimming pulled off such Christmas candles. I am quite unequal to the part of villain myself, or I'd gi'e all my small silver to see that lady toppered" (p. 308). The skimmington has been interpreted as a symbolic expression by society of its rejection of the corruption in Henchard, as retribution for his violation of the sanctity of social order in selling his

wife (for example, see Paterson, "*The Mayor of Casterbridge* as Tragedy," pp. 159, 167-70). This symbolic reading may be accurate if we grant the symbolists' suggestion that Henchard is, by virtue of his social stature in a traditional hierarchic society, responsible for the depraved condition of Mixen Lane. But Henchard is not referred to by the skimmington organizers: it is Lucetta explicitly whom the ride is directed toward, and to a lesser extent Farfrae, whose eventual destruction in the cyclic pattern is foreshadowed by the skimmington. The skimmington has no implication to Henchard's sale of his wife; it is, as Mrs. Cuxsom tells Newsom in Peter's Finger tavern, a "foolish thing they do in these parts when a man's wife is — well, not too particularly his own" (p. 300). Since Henchard has already been toppled, it is evidently felt by the denizens of Mixen Lane that mockery of his sexual morality will make no difference to him — as indeed it does not. After a temporary concern for Elizabeth-Jane's reaction, he attempts to help the prostrated Lucetta by locating Farfrae (pp. 327 ff.). Contrary to Paterson's belief that the lower classes of Mixen Lane express a group morality that must cast Henchard from Casterbridge as Oedipus was cast from Thebes (Paterson, p. 163), their expression of moral outrage is directed explicitly toward Lucetta. "'Mrs. Farfrae wrote [those letters, which Jopp has just read]!' said Nance Mockridge. ''Tis a humbling thing for us, as respectable women, that one of the same sex could do it. And now she's vowed herself to another man!'" (p. 298). The furmity woman, whose denunciation of Henchard as magistrate marked the point where Henchard's decline increased precipitously, also voices resentment against Lucetta as a justification for the skimmington, though perhaps ironically: "Ah, I saved her from a real bad marriage [with Henchard, by revealing he had sold his first wife], and she's never been the one to thank me" (p. 298).

12. See, for example, Robert B. Heilman's introduction to *The Mayor of Casterbridge*, Riverside ed. (Boston: Houghton Mifflin, 1962), p. xxv.


## CHAPTER FIVE

1. The best-known expression of this idea is Donald Davidson, "The Trational Basis of Thomas Hardy's Fiction," *Southern Review*, 6 (1940): 162-78.

2. Among the attempts to define the special bent of *The Woodlanders* are Robert Y. Drake, Jr., "*The Woodlanders* as Traditional Pastoral," *MFS* 6 (1960): 251-57; William H. Matchett, "*The Woodlanders*, or Realism in Sheep's Clothing," *NCF* 9 (1955): 241-61. Eugene Goodheart, "Thomas Hardy and the Lyrical Novel," *NCF* 12 (1957): 215-25, relies mainly on this one novel to illustrate a manner of writing that "sheds the social surface

and shows us the naked emotion" (p. 218). Beach's chapter on *The Wood-landers* in *The Technique of Thomas Hardy*, pp. 158-76, is an intelligent and literate summary of its formal qualities, although I obviously do not concur in his estimate that *The Woodlanders* is "a failure in technique" (p. 165).

3. Carpenter, *Thomas Hardy*, pp. 123-24, attributes the novel's "Sophoclean grandeur" to its infusion "with anthropological significance that broadens and deepens its social and psychological themes. . . . it is far from a Greek tragedy; but it is based on the same mythic foundation as were the dramas of Sophocles and Aeschylus."

4. *On a Darkling Plain*, p. 167.

5. See George Levine, "Determinism and Responsibility in the Works of George Eliot," *PMLA* 77 (1962): 268-79, for a discussion of the different implications of determinism and fatalism in literary works [see also chap. 1, n18].

6. George S. Fayen, Jr., "Hardy's *The Woodlanders*: Inwardness and Memory," *SEL* 1, 4 (1961): 91.

7. See my "Revisions and Vision: Thomas Hardy's *The Woodlanders*," *BNYPL* 75 (1971): 250-55.

8. A continual point of contention among readers of Hardy is whether Giles's self-sacrifice is admirable or foolish. A recent argument for the former view is Brooks, *Thomas Hardy*, pp. 8, 227-32; for the latter view, Peter J. Casagrande, "The Shifted 'Centre of Altruism' in *The Woodlanders:* Thomas Hardy's Third 'Return of a Native,'" *ELH* 38 (1971): 122.

9. Hardy's judgment of Grace is reported by Rebekah Owen: "He said that Grace never interested him much; he was provoked with her all along. If she would have done a really self-abandoned, impassioned thing (gone off with Giles), he could have made a fine tragic ending to the book, but she was too commonplace and straitlaced and he could not make her." Quoted by Carl J. Weber, *Hardy and the Lady from Madison Square* (Waterville, Maine: Colby College Press, 1952), p. 89. This opinion, which seems to be an authorial refutation of my contention that the novel is a successful tragedy, overlooks a crucial point, possibly because it was offered casually in 1893, years after he had written the novel in its major, unalterable outlines. The likelihood that Giles would have defied his household laws by adultery and elopement is even less plausible than that Grace would have been able to break with her staid past. Owen succinctly and accurately replied to Hardy that Grace was "willin'" when Giles was not.

10. For example, Beach, *The Technique of Thomas Hardy*, pp. 164-73; Howe, *Thomas Hardy*, p. 103; Carpenter, *Thomas Hardy*, p. 114.

11. "*The Mayor of Casterbridge* as Tragedy."

12. See my "Revisions and Vision," p. 223.


## CHAPTER SIX

1. *Tess of the d'Urbervilles* has elicited many general observations about its tragic atmosphere and action but few appraisals of the techniques that invest the story with the potentiality of tragedy. Most critics refer to the grand simplicity of Tess Durbeyfield struggling to remain true to her finer human impulses in face of her powerful adversaries; she must battle Chance and the "President of the Immortals" and her own passionate inclinations, as well as social conventions which can both cripple the personality of Angel Clare and expel Tess's family from the community. These views may be found in the following critical works, usually with more complex ramifications than my brief summary may suggest: Beach, *The Technique of Thomas Hardy*, pp. 206-12; William R. Rutland, *Thomas Hardy: A Study of His Writings and Their Background* (Oxford: Basil Blackwell, 1938), pp. 230-38; Weber, *Hardy of Wessex* (1940), pp. 132-33; Webster, *On a Darkling Plain*, pp. 173-80; Ian Gregor, "The Novel as Moral Protest: *Tess of the d'Urbervilles*," in Gregor and Nicholas, *The Moral and the Story* (London: Faber and Faber, 1962), pp. 136-41; J.I.M. Stewart, "Hardy," *Eight Modern Writers*, The Oxford History of English Literature 12 (Oxford: Clarendon, 1963): 42-44; Howe, *Thomas Hardy*, pp. 108-32, esp. pp. 129-32. A more specialized thesis by James Hazen, "The Tragedy of Tess Durbeyfield," *TSLL* 11 (1969): 779-94, traces the pattern of a "scapegoat tragedy" through the novel.

2. See my "Marlow, Myth, and Structure in *Lord Jim*," *Criticism* 8 (1966): 263-79.

3. David Lodge, *Language of Fiction: Essays in Criticism and Verbal Analysis of the English Novel* (London: Routledge and Kegan Paul; New York: Columbia Univ. Press, 1966), pp. 176-79, analyzes page 108 of *Tess of the d'Urbervilles* where the statement "the world is only a psychological phenomenon" is made, but his demand that fiction present a unified view of reality causes him to react quite differently to Hardy's impressionism from the way I do. "The reader must be able to identify this consciousness [of the focus of narration], and he does so by responding correctly to the language used. The case against Hardy is that he regularly confuses the

reader with a number of conflicting linguistic clues" (p. 179). Lodge emphasizes tone and level of vocabulary. His demurral is evidence that even a reader exceptionally alert to nuances of language can fail to see the overall functionalism of apparent inconsistencies. For a theory of point of view that substantiates the insistence of Lodge and of Bernard J. Paris, "'A Confusion of Many Standards': Conflicting Value Systems in *Tess of the d'Urbervilles*," *NCF* 24 (1969): 57-79, that a novel present a unified and definable authorial morality, see Wayne C. Booth, *The Rhetoric of Fiction* (Chicago: Univ. of Chicago Press, 1961), chaps. 11-13.

4. See, for example, Lucille Herbert, "Hardy's Views in *Tess of the d'Urbervilles*," *ELH* 37 (1970):90; for a summary of philosophical contradictions in the novel, see Michael Millgate, *Thomas Hardy: His Career as a Novelist* (New York: Random House, 1971), pp. 270-71. An intelligent if somewhat rigid and generally unsympathetic analysis of Hardy's efforts to establish a value-system or morality is Bernard J. Paris, "'A Confusion of Many Standards,'" pp. 57-59.

5. Lodge, pp. 177-78.

6. Bert G. Hornback, *The Metaphor of Chance: Vision and Technique in the Works of Thomas Hardy* (Athens: Ohio Univ. Press, 1971), discusses the centralness of Hardy's intensity through a large part of his work. He is concerned primarily with the creation in the reader of a sense of intensity by means of compressed time, allusions to history, and repetitions rather than with the quality of intense consciousness in the protagonists; see p. 124, for his comment about p. 160 of *Tess of the d'Urbervilles*.

7. The two kinds of mystical experience which the last paragraph indicates Tess was capable of are similar to those experienced by Alfred Tennyson. Tennyson claimed to be able by repeating his name to induce a "waking trance," in which "all at once, as it were out of the intensity of the consciousness of individuality, the individuality itself seemed to dissolve and fade away into boundless being,...the loss of personality (if so it were) seeming no extinction but the only true life." Quoted by Hallam Tennyson in *Alfred Lord Tennyson: A Memoir by His Son* (London: Macmillan, 1897), I: 320. His one profound experience is described in *In Memoriam*, lyric 95; ibid., 2:90. Though Hallam Tennyson's biography of his father was not published until 1897, it is not unlikely that Hardy would have heard of these "visions," and of course he knew *In Memoriam*. "The Ancient Sage" also portrays a mystical state.

8. Dorothy Van Ghent, *The English Novel: Form and Function* (New York: Rinehart, 1953), pp. 200-1.

9. Lodge, p. 185.

10. In an 1892 interview, Hardy says that Tess had to die, that she could not have been reconciled with Angel because "he would have inevitably thrown her fall in her face." *Book Buyer* 9 (1892): 153. Hardy expressed essentially the same idea a few months later: see Raymond Blathwayt, "A Chat with the Author of 'Tess,'" *Black and White*, 27 August 1892 (reprinted in *Thomas Hardy and His Readers*, p. 92). Though Angel is far from perfection at the novel's end, a future rejection of Tess is made to seem less inevitable than, say, Fitzpiers's eventual infidelity to Grace.

11. See J. O. Bailey, *The Poetry of Thomas Hardy: A Handbook and Commentary* (Chapel Hill: Univ. of North Carolina Press, 1970), pp. 154-55, for a survey of similar passages of idealistic delusion in Hardy's novels. Bailey considers them in relation to "The Well-Beloved" motif in Hardy, which suggests that an Ideal beauty exists but only in the eye of the beholder. The novel *The Well-Beloved* was conceived during the writing of *Tess of the d'Urbervilles* (Purdy, *Thomas Hardy*, p. 94), an indication that Hardy's interest in subjective life was not exhausted by writing the greater novel.

12. Schweik in "Moral Perspective" discusses the lack of a final truth in the novel; see also F.R. Southerington, *Hardy's Vision of Man* (London: Chatto and Windus, 1971), p. 125.

13. For example, see Johnson, *The Art of Thomas Hardy*, pp. 220-25, 234-35, 243-45; Holloway, "Hardy's Major Fiction," pp. 243-44; Van Ghent, p. 201.

14. For example, William McCollum, *Tragedy* (New York: Macmillan, 1957), p. 60; Raymond Williams, *Modern Tragedy* (Stanford: Stanford Univ. Press, 1966), pp. 61-84; Richmond Y. Hathorn, *Tragedy, Myth, and Mystery* (Bloomington: Indiana Univ. Press, 1962), pp. 11-37.

15. J. Hillis Miller's critical writings deal often, and in various ways, with a concept of subjectivity. He most closely approximates my analysis of *Tess of the d'Urbervilles* when he writes, "Nothing now [in post-Nietzschean philosophy] has any worth except the arbitrary value [man] sets on things as he assimilates them into his consciousness. . . . In the emptiness left after the death of God, man becomes the sovereign valuer, the measure of all things." *Poets of Reality: Six Twentieth-Century Writers* (Cambridge, Mass.: Harvard Univ. Press, Belknap Press, 1965), pp. 3-4. There are certain clear parallels between Miller's theory and *Tess of the d'Urbervilles*; most pertinently, perhaps, whatever grandeur there is in Tess's suffering comes because we are forced to see her suffering in a world that offers no supernatural consolation and sets no supernatural values. On the other hand, the subjectivity in *Tess of the d'Urbervilles* is as akin to "classical" mysti-

cism of intense introspection as it is to the *Weltanschauung* that Miller's
literary theories are based on. It is not necessary to elevate Tess into a
cultural marker, as one would need to do if Miller's lead were followed to
its logical ends, in order to explain adequately the power she exerts upon
our sympathy. However, for Miller's opinion as to the manner in which a
subjectivist outlook may lead to a *Weltanschauung*, see his *The Disappearance of God* (Cambridge, Mass.: Harvard Univ. Press, Belknap Press, 1963),
esp. pp. 7, 10, 11.


## CHAPTER SEVEN

1. This increasing personal quality was noticed by some of the early reviewers of *Jude the Obscure*; see Edmund Gosse, *Cosmopolis*, January
1896 (reprinted in *Thomas Hardy and His Readers*, p. 121). The reviewer
for the *Bookman* (London), January 1896 (*Thomas Hardy and His Readers*,
p. 130), calls *Jude the Obscure* "downright propaganda." Richard Le Gal-
lienne, in *The Idler*, February 1896 (*Thomas Hardy and His Readers*, p.
137), describes the novel as a "masterly piece of special pleading."

2. Zabel, Introduction, *Jude the Obscure*, Collier ed. (New York: Macmillan,
1962), p. 17. See also Stewart, *Eight Modern Writers*, pp. 43-44; Guerard,
*Thomas Hardy*, pp. 153-57; Norman Holland, Jr., "*Jude the Obscure*:
Hardy's Symbolic Indictment of Christianity," *NCF* 9 (1954): 50, 57-58.
Another view, complementary to my analysis of authorial distance, is Robert B. Heilman, Introduction, *Jude the Obscure*, Perennial ed. (New York:
Harper & Row, 1966), pp. 6-14 et passim. Heilman points out the inconsistencies among "philosophic" ideas in the novel, and notes that "the marriage theme is dominated not by the social criticism voiced by the characters but by Hardy's psychological awareness, his sense of Jude's and Sue's
own natures" (p. 13).

3. Weber, *Hardy of Wessex* (1965), p. 206.

4. Barbara Hardy, *The Appropriate Form: An Essay on the Novel* (London:
Athlone Press of the Univ. of London), pp. 70-73, 82.

5. Arthur Mizener, "The Novel of Doctrine in the Nineteenth Century:
Hardy's *Jude the Obscure*," pp. 55-77; this is a refinement of his earlier
"*Jude the Obscure* as a Tragedy," *Southern Review* 6 (1940): 193-213.

6. "*Jude the Obscure* as a Tragedy," p. 197, n7; p. 201. For a different analysis of a limitation in Mizener's approach, see Ted R. Spivey, "Thomas
Hardy's Tragic Hero," *NCF* 9 (1954): 179-91.

7. J. Hillis Miller, *Thomas Hardy: Distance and Desire* (Cambridge: Harvard Univ. Press, Belknap Press, 1970), pp. 214-16, suggests a variation upon this idea. Miller says that Hardy's novels show an increasing convergence of the protagonist's and the narrator's points of view: "In the novels this convergence is never complete, but the understanding of Jude just before his death more nearly approaches the narrator's understanding than does the understanding of earlier heroes like Eustacia [see chap. 3, n12] or Henchard." Miller's biases are quite different from mine; he sees Hardy primarily as a thinker who more and more directly articulates his ideas by means of the novels' denouements, while I see Hardy becoming more of an experimentalist whose use of a variety of devices separates the ideas he articulates from himself. A position similar to Miller's is Daniel R. Schwarz, "The Narrator as Character in Hardy's Major Fiction," *MFS* 18(1972): 155-72.

8. Indeed, this experience of Jude's is almost identical to one of Hardy's youthful memories included in his autobiography (*Early Life*, pp. 19-20).

9. Evidence that Hardy did intentionally, rather than uncontrollably, initiate the presentation of Jude in this abrupt fashion is the description of Little Father Time after he commits suicide. Jude reports to Sue the opinion of the examining doctor, an "advanced man," in words that echo back to young Jude's ruminations: "They [i.e., youths] seem to see all [of life's] terrors before they are old enough to have staying power to resist them. He says it is the beginning of the coming universal wish not to live" (p. 406). And the long course of the novel's composition hardly supports the image of Hardy writing at white heat. The idea for the novel was conceived in 1887, the "scheme" jotted down in 1890; the plot was outlined in 1892 and 1893, the story finally written out in 1893 and 1894. The anger that the novel projects is certainly intended, and very skillfully managed.

10. Ward Hellstrom, "Hardy's Use of Setting and *Jude the Obscure*," *VNL*, no. 25 (1964): 11-13.

11. See "How Shall We Solve the Divorce Problem?" *Nash's Magazine*, March 1912, p. 683; excerpted in *Thomas Hardy's Personal Writings*, ed. Orel, p. 252.

12. For example, Beach, The *Technique of Thomas Hardy*, pp. 234-35; Carl J. Weber, Introduction, *Jude the Obscure*, Modern Classics ed. (New York: Harper, 1957), p. xvii.

13. For example, Grant Allen, *English Barbarians* (London: J. Lane, 1895), pp. 175-79, who argues (as does Hardy) that marriage should be dissolved on the wish of either partner.

14. Many readers of *Jude the Obscure* have pointed to the presentation of Little Father Time as a glaring indication of Hardy's indifference to plausibility. They feel that Hardy's main interest in writing the novel was to attack social injustice and to attract sympathy for people whose lives were stunted by social wrongs. (Certainly Little Father Time's desperate longing for stability and security is explained by his early life during which he had been sent from home to home.) I would agree that Little Father Time is not satisfactorily handled: with him Hardy takes the methods of distancing that I am discussing as far as they can be taken, and indeed beyond their effectiveness. But I am not particularly disturbed by Hardy's grotesque introduction of Little Father Time on the train as "Age masquerading as Juvenility" and as "an enslaved and dwarfed Divinity" (p. 332). This introduction shares many aspects of Hardy's characteristic abruptness, whose function in *Jude the Obscure* I have already discussed; thereafter, Hardy generally allows other characters to refer to Little Father Time's symbolic aspects, and the narrator's views do not become obtrusive. Hardy fails with Little Father Time because he never gives him anything to do in the novel, until of course the boy performs the novel's most striking physical action. He is only baggage to be taken wherever Sue and Jude move; he does not contribute to the novel's sense of ongoing living. Hardy's failure to develop Little Father Time helps to explain the hollowness in the suicide note that is his rationalization to the outside world: *"Done because we are too menny"* (p. 405). In content this is similar to the recollection by the dying Jude of the Book of Job—*"There* [in death] *the prisoners rest together; they hear not the voice of the oppressor"* (p. 488)—but the suicide note has none of the resonance of final knowledge or final discovery. Jude like Little Father Time had entered the novel abruptly, with an already formed, individualistic frame of mind. But Jude's mind evolves, and by the time he dies the reader has seen a person being shaped by experience: with Little Father Time there has been only generalization *about* experience.

15. My views here are opposed to those of Dorothy Van Ghent and other critics that Hardy's fiction is divisible into concrete narrative (which they consider genuine) and abstract philosophizing (which they consider artificial and imposed upon the "real" story). Van Ghent, *The English Novel*, p. 196 et passim; Arnold Kettle, *An Introduction to the English Novel* (London: Hutchinson, 1953), 2: 60-61; Douglas Brown, *Thomas Hardy* (London: Longmans, 1954), pp. 119-21; Carpenter, *Thomas Hardy*, pp. 22-23. Though their remarks have value in indicating the breach between the storyteller and his tale, their criticisms of Hardy for his two kinds of language, or for the conflict between the narrator and the fiction's concrete demonstration, are shortsighted. The view advanced by Robert Schweik, "Moral Perspective in *Tess of the d'Urbervilles*," pp. 14, 18, is more defensible—that the full meaning of a work of art cannot be understood by ignoring a major linguistic element. See also the eloquent argument for

pluralistic readings of literature by Robert Heilman, "Hardy's 'Mayor' and the Problem of Intention," *Criticism* 5 (1963): 199-213: and Lodge, *Language of Fiction*, p. 168.

16. Richard Benvenuto, "Modes of Perception: The Will to Live in *Jude the Obscure*," *Studies in the Novel* 2 (1970): 31-41, argues that the narrator's views are distinctive and separate from those of characters and of Hardy himself.

17. The narrator says that Gillingham's advice is "good," implying a distance between Phillotson's ethical conscientiousness and the narrator's views. But the word may be an ironic adjective, that is, "good" as conventional or well-meant, but inadequate. On the next page, the narrator says that the theater people act "nobly" in defending Phillotson at the hearing. These passages further suggest a lack of clear preference within the text of the novel.

18. For example, Howe, *Thomas Hardy*, p. 21; Janet Burstein, "The Journey beyond Myth in *Jude the Obscure*," *TSLL* 15 (1973): 502-4.

19. Millgate, *Thomas Hardy*, pp. 324-25, considers several classical echoes and allusions in *Jude the Obscure;* some he thinks are at least partly ironic.

20. Samuel Hynes, *The Pattern of Hardy's Poetry* (Chapel Hill: Univ. of North Carolina Press, 1961). Hynes analyzes such irreconcilable opposites as hope and despair in "The Darkling Thrush," iceberg (Nature's blind force) and ship (man's aspirations) in "The Convergence of the Twain."

21. William J. Hyde, "Theoretic and Practical Unconventionality in *Jude the Obscure*," *NCF* 20 (1965): 163. Hyde quotes Mill's "Of Individuality": "The pattern that an individual chooses 'is the best, not because it is the best in itself, but because it is his own mode.'"

# INDEX

Abel, Lionel, 169
Abercrombie, Lascelles, 20
Aeschylus, 162, 177
Allen, Grant, 182
*Ambassadors, The,* 80-81
"Ancient Sage, The," 179
Aninism: in *Madding Crowd,* 36;
  in *Woodlanders,* 94-96, 106: in
  *Tess,* 119, 133-34: in *Jude,* 151.
  *See also* Correspondence
*Antigone,* 50, 96, 114, 115
Aristotle, 12, 14, 42, 70, 84, 162, 170,
  175. *See also* Tragedy, classical
Arnold, Matthew, 168
*Autobiography* (J.S. Mill), 168
Authorial voice. *See* Narrator: Point
  of view

Bailey, J.O., 180
Benvenuto, Richard, 172, 184
Beach, Joseph Warren, 14-15n11,
  20, 45n9, 177

*Belgravia,* 174
Bible, The, 10, 12
Blathwayt, Raymond, 180
*Book Buyer,* 180
*Bookman,* 181
Booth, Wayne C., 179
Bradley, A.C., 14
*Bride of Lammermoor, The,* 10
Brontë, Charlotte, 137
Brooks, Jean, 166, 177

Carpenter, Richard C., 45, 63, 177
Casagrande, Peter J., 177
Cecil, David, 167
Chance, 14, 18, 35, 178
Characterization: undercharacter-
  ization common in Hardy, 61-62,
  140, 143, 183; dramatic (objective)
  aspect of, 63, 78, 144-49 passim;
  lack of villains, 93, 96, 106, 109,
— , TH's management of: in *Madding
  Crowd,* 9, 25-34 passim,46; in

185

Dale Kramer is professor of English at the University of Illinois at Urbana-Champaign. He received his M.A. (1960) and Ph.D. (1963) degrees from Western Reserve University. Articles by Dr. Kramer have appeared in various scholarly journals, and his book Charles Robert Maturin was published in 1973.

The manuscript was edited by Marguerite C. Wallace. The book was designed by Gil Hanna. The typeface for the text is English; and the display face is Helvetica designed by Max Miedinger.

The text is printed on Nicolet Natural text paper; and the book is bound in Holliston's Payko over binders' boards. Manufactured in the United States of America.